DOLE QUEUES AND D

Dole Queues
and Demons

British Election Posters from the Conservative Party Archive

STUART BALL

Bodleian Library
UNIVERSITY OF OXFORD

ACKNOWLEDGEMENTS

Thanks are due to Patricia Brown for the generous financial support
which has made publication of this book possible, and to Nigel Chivers
for his guidance in the development of the book and its contents.

First published in 2011 by the Bodleian Library
Broad Street
Oxford OX1 3BG

www.bodleianbookshop.co.uk

ISBN 978 185124 353 2

Foreword © Maurice Saatchi
Text © Stuart Ball
Photography © Conservative Party Archive Trust, 2011
Brick wall image on back panel © Scott Latham–Fotolia.com

Cover design by Dot Little
Designed and typeset in 11 on 16 point Monotype Ehrhardt and Gotham Bold
by illuminati, Grosmont
Printed and bound on 157 gsm Gold East matte art paper
by Great Wall Printing, China

British Library Catalogue in Publishing Data
A CIP record of this publication is available from the British Library

CONTENTS

THE LIGHTHOUSE OF CONSERVATISM (1929)

One of a series of colourful posters produced for the general election of 1929.

1929/35

PREFACE

Twitter, Facebook, soundbites, the Internet – all have their place in modern political communications but none comes close to creating the memorable impact of a well-crafted poster. At the Conservative Party Archive, housed in the Bodleian Library, Oxford, we have over 650 such posters spanning the twentieth century to the present day. Witty, skilfully produced and often bitingly savage, they have raised awareness of issues, vilified political opponents and pushed the Conservative Party line.

This collection represents the pick of the crop. We are indebted to Maurice Saatchi, whose role in redefining posters as a primary means of communication cannot be overestimated, for his perceptive thoughts. Throughout the book, Stuart Ball's knowledgeable and readable introductions and captions put the posters into historical and political perspective.

It is interesting to track the parallels of political posters and mainstream commercial advertising, from the artwork posters of the early twentieth century, through the privations of the Second World War, to today's media-savvy presentations. While the personality of political leaders – from Baldwin to Cameron – has remained a constant theme, many of the issues addressed by earlier posters such as 'Safeguarding' and 'Free Trade' are now just distant memories. The posters span a period of changing views and opinions; times when political correctness did not mean the same as it does today. To modern eyes, many of the posters will appear insulting or xenophobic, but they are part of history.

Lastly, my thanks for buying this book. The work of the Conservative Party Archive is funded by trustees, and profits from sales of this book will make a valuable contribution to our work at the Bodleian.

Dr Philip Brown
Chairman of the Trustees, Conservative Party Archive

NEW LABOUR NEW DANGER

One of Labour's leaders, Clare Short, says dark forces behind Tony Blair manipulate policy in a sinister way. "I sometimes call them the people who live in the dark." She says about New Labour: "It's a lie. And it's dangerous."

NEW LABOUR, NEW DANGER (1997)

The idea for this iconic poster, used in the 1997 general election, came from a press picture of the Labour leader, Tony Blair, with demon eyes taped across it, which a member of staff at Conservative Central Office had stuck to a waste-paper basket as a joke.

1997–08

FOREWORD

Posters are to politics what poetry is to literature: the only possible words in the only possible order.

They should instantly convey the core message in a memorable way. This requires a handful of words, each of which is perfectly chosen, married to an image which reinforces them. When this happens posters can be the single defining medium of a campaign.

It is vital that the core message of a poster is clear and simple. It must relate to the whole of the political campaign, and the ideology behind it.

These characteristics are similar, but not identical, to commercial posters. Commercial poster campaigns are part of complete marketing strategies, whether for a short period or many years of brand building. Political posters work best when they come straight to the point – no vagueness, waffle or flimflam. Just one message with one idea illustrated by one simple fact.

Those designing political poster campaigns have some options which are not available for commercial use, such as negative messages and/or personal attacks. 'Negative campaigning' is inevitable – because general elections are intellectual battles in which the winner is the one with the best arguments, not the prettiest face. It is the duty of the leader of any party seeking election to point out the defects in their opponents' position.

The Conservative Party Archive, from which these posters have been selected, displays the development of the political poster. The early ones were produced and used in a very different media climate from our own. First radio and then television altered the political scene, and recent developments of social media have altered it again. Political campaigners these days have far more choices of how to convey their message. But posters remain an important vehicle whereas some other forms of campaigning have changed out of recognition or vanished like the hundreds of local, regional and national political meetings that were held a few decades ago.

The collection reflects changing artistic styles as well as the changing political environment. It also reflects changing political priorities. Some of the messages have a modern feel – 'Don't let Labour ruin it' and 'It's time for a change' (first used in 1951). Others refer to issues that no longer feature, such as tariff reform, which has been replaced by controversy about the EU.

I commend this fascinating collection of over a century of Conservative posters to all those interested in election campaigning. Political posters deserve a place on your bookshelf, alongside your poetry.

THE PEOPLE'S BUDGET

Our century of posters begins in the Edwardian era, not long before the outbreak of the First World War in 1914. These pre-war years were a troubled time for the Conservative Party; in a similar way to the period from 1997 to 2010, which closes this volume, there were internal divisions and problems in finding an attractive programme, and the result was a series of election defeats. In 1902, Arthur Balfour succeeded his uncle, Lord Salisbury, as prime minister and leader of the Conservative Party. However, his government ran into increasing problems, and ended with the most serious defeat that the Conservative Party has suffered in the last 150 years. There were difficulties and disputes over a range of issues at home and overseas, but by far the most damage was done by the question of 'tariff reform'.

This explosive topic was raised in May 1903 by the next most powerful figure in the government, Joseph Chamberlain, and at once it transformed the political landscape. His proposal was to introduce protectionist tariff duties on imports entering Britain, but to give a lower preferential rate to goods from the Empire and thus advantage them over the foreigner. In return, the now self-governing dominions, such as Canada, would give British exports a similar preference in their domestic markets. Chamberlain's purpose was to bring the Empire into a closer economic unity, and so preserve Britain's position as a world power against advancing rivals. The tariff reform programme gained the support of many Conservatives, as it had the crucial combination of an appeal to both the pocket and the heart. The purely protectionist aspect would help those sectors of British industry which were struggling with foreign competition, and it also offered the prospect that the revenue from the tariff duties would finance such social reforms as old-age pensions – avoiding the need for any increase in direct taxation, which Conservatives considered had reached its practical limits. The imperial aspect of the policy struck a resonant chord with Conservative ideals, and many younger figures took up the cause with passionate commitment.

However, tariff reform also had great political drawbacks. The simplest of these was that it entailed a radical change from the established policy of free trade, which had been in place since the abandonment of protectionism in the 1840s. For many, free trade was almost unquestionable as the foundation of Britain's industrial growth and pre-eminence as a worldwide trading nation. The biggest electoral problem resulted from the fact that most of the Empire produce was raw materials and food, and any suggestion of introducing tariffs on food imports alarmed urban working-class voters over the potential rise in the cost of living. At once, the Liberal Party raised the cry of 'food taxes' and 'stomach taxes', with images of a return to early-nineteenth-century poverty. In vain did the supporters of tariff reform argue that free trade was the main cause of unemployment, allowing foreign countries to 'dump' goods, due to surpluses or subsidies, into the British market at prices with which domestic manufacturers could not compete. Their claim that protectionist tariffs would lead to prosperity, security of employment and higher wage levels drew some working-class support, but many more voters feared the effects of the change.

The unpopularity of tariff reform was the main cause of the Liberal Party's landslide victory in the general election of January 1906. In 1900, the Conservatives and their Liberal Unionist partners had won 402 seats and the Liberal Party only 183; now, that was more than reversed, with the Unionist alliance slumping to 156 seats, whilst the Liberals won 399 and their supporters, the Irish Nationalists and the infant Labour Party, won 82 and 29 seats respectively. However, although the Liberals had a massive majority in the House of Commons, they faced the problem that the Unionists had a similarly large preponderance in the House of Lords. Between 1906 and 1909, Balfour and the leader of the Unionist alliance in the upper chamber, Lord Lansdowne, used this advantage to throw out or render useless many of the reform measures which the Liberals brought forward. In 1908, shortly before he became prime minister, Herbert

Asquith's budget introduced free old-age pensions, but apart from this the Liberal government seemed to be stumbling towards another defeat. Instead, in the following year Conservative expectations were thwarted by the ingenuity of Asquith's successor as chancellor of the exchequer, David Lloyd George.

Lloyd George framed his first budget in the spring of 1909 as a deliberate political challenge to the Conservatives, the House of Lords and tariff reform. Calling it 'the People's Budget', he included the key financial provisions from the previously mangled Liberal bills, and he found the additional money needed to finance both the old-age pensions and the accelerating naval race with Germany by introducing the super-tax – a higher rate tax band for the largest incomes. Most importantly, the budget demolished a key argument for tariff reform: that orthodox free-trade fiscal measures had reached their limits. After further provocation from Lloyd George's radical oratory, the Conservatives responded by throwing out the budget when it reached the House of Lords in late 1909. They claimed that this was not against constitutional precedent, and that the Lords were actually performing a valuable democratic role in blocking measures for which there was no popular mandate and forcing an appeal to the electorate.

The Conservative campaign against the 'People's Budget' was not carried out directly by the party organisation, but instead a special body was set up: the 'Budget Protest League'. This was not really independent – it was presided over by one of the party's leaders, Walter Long, and it worked closely with Conservative Central Office. The posters in this chapter are selected from the many produced by the Budget Protest League between the summer of 1909 and the general election that followed the Lords' rejection of the budget, which took place in January 1910. The posters therefore mainly concentrate on the defects of the budget, both in its specific provisions and in its general effects. Two key themes are the vulnerability of the free-trade economy to foreign competition, with the iconic figure of 'John Bull' bereft of any weapons of defence or retaliation, and the consequent unemployment, leading to misery and improverishment for British workers. As the author of the budget, Lloyd George figures in these posters rather than Asquith, the prime minister and Liberal leader.

The final posters in the selection come from the January 1910 election campaign, which was fought as much on the issue of tariff reform versus free trade as on the constitutional position of the House of Lords. They illustrate the electoral problems which the Conservatives faced, and the extent to which they were on the defensive.

In January 1910 the Conservatives recovered many of the safer seats lost in 1906, but were unable to prise the Liberals from office. They won 272 seats to the Liberals' 274, but Asquith remained securely in power due to the support of the 40 Labour MPs and, most of all, the 82 Irish Nationalists. After the election, the Conservatives accepted the verdict on the 'People's Budget' and the House of Lords passed it unamended – but now the struggle turned to the powers of the upper chamber itself. Resolving this constitutional crisis required a further general election in December 1910, which had almost identical results; following this, under the threat of a mass creation of Liberal peers, the House of Lords passed the Parliament Act in 1911. This greatly reduced its powers, and paved the way to the bitter struggle over Irish Home Rule which dominated British politics from 1912 to the outbreak of the First World War in August 1914.

**LLOYD GEORGE'S SAUCE
(1909)**

The poster refers to the existing duties on some items of food and drink (especially beer and spirits), as part of the debate over tariff reform versus free trade.

1909/10–11

THE PEERS TO THE PEOPLE:-
"HULLO, ARE YOU THERE? WE ARE WAITING FOR INSTRUCTIONS."

THE PEERS TO THE PEOPLE (1909)

This justifies the rejection of the 'People's Budget' by the House of Lords as a democratic action of referral to the electorate, and suggests that the peers are simply servants of the people; the peer on the telephone bears some resemblance to Lord Lansdowne, the Conservative leader in the House of Lords.

1909/10-25

AT THE POLL (1910)

This refers to the loss of many Liberal seats in the general election of January 1910; however, the result still left the Liberal government in power.

1909/10-28

TAFFY WAS A WELSHMAN (1910)

Playing on popular prejudice and a well-known contemporary nursery rhyme (the missing word in the couplet being 'thief'), the poster refutes the idea that Lloyd George deserved any credit for the surplus in his budget of 1910.

1909/10-31

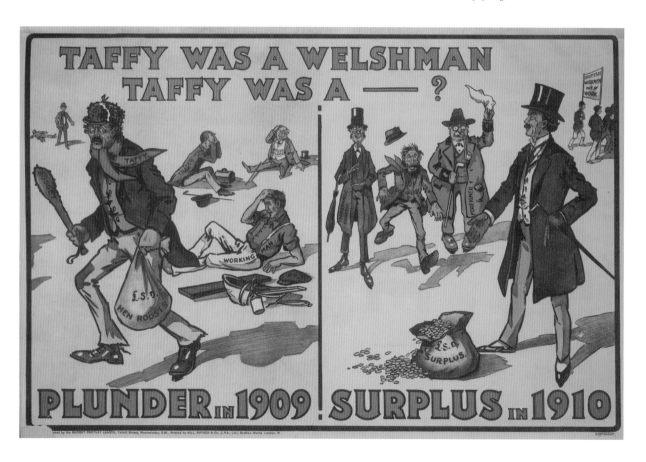

LESS BEER, LESS BACCY, LESS EMPLOYMENT (1909)

This refers to the increases in tobacco and alcohol duties which were part of Lloyd George's measures to increase revenue.

1909/10–16

14

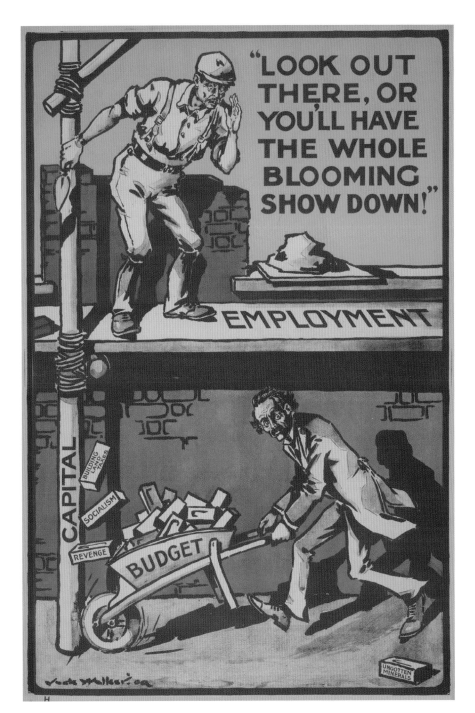

LOOK OUT THERE (1909)

This develops the Conservative argument that the 'People's Budget' was a reckless attack on capital, and would increase unemployment rather than reduce it.

1909/10-13

AN ENGLISHMAN'S HOME
(1909)

1909/10-21

THE FRAUD EXPOSED! (1909)

1909/10-29

SOCIALISM THROTTLING THE COUNTRY (1909)

In this period, the term 'socialism' was used by Conservatives to criticise the interventionist measures of the Liberal government, and was not aimed at the very small Labour Party.

1909/10-14

GET OFF THE EARTH! (1909)

The emblematic figure of
John Bull is shown as being
defenceless against foreign
competition in his own country,
due to the binding effect of the
free-trade system.

1909/10–12

THE MERRY WIDOW (1909)

The widow has the face of
Asquith, the Liberal prime
minister, whilst the 'dumper'
is portrayed in the way of
contemporary caricatures of
Germans, Germany being
Britain's main commercial
competitor.

1909/10–17

BRITONS, HELP! (1909)

The emblematic figures of a Frenchman (in top hat), a German (in brown coat), an American (depicted as 'Uncle Sam') and a Russian eject the defenceless John Bull from the world's markets.

1909/10-23

THE PEOPLE'S BUDGET! (1909)

The comment of the 'Genial Foreigner' refers to the Tariff Reform alternative to unrestricted free trade, suggesting that taxes on foreign imports would protect employment.

1909/10-27

CHINAMAN NO LIKEE
EAT SICK PIG

He makee velly good
FLEE TLADE ENGLISH BACON

**CHINAMAN NO LIKEE
EAT SICK PIG (1909)**

The poster uses contemporary
racial stereotypes, which would
not be considered acceptable
today, to underline the dangers
of unrestricted free imports.

1909/10-26

THE END OF THE LLOYD GEORGE BUDGET (1909)

This poster showing a working man's rejection of the 'People's Budget' in favour of tariff reform and more employment was premature; after the Liberal government won the general election of January 1910, the House of Lords conceded and the budget was passed without any amendment.

1909/10–20A

NOTICE
OLD-AGE PENSIONS
WILL BE CONTINUED
BY THE
UNIONISTS
ARTHUR JAMES BALFOUR

Issued by THE PENNY BUDGET, Caxton House (East Bloc), Westminster, London, S.W., and Printed by St. Clements Press, Ltd., Portugal St., London, W.C.

OLD-AGE PENSIONS (1910)

This poster from the January 1910 general election illustrates the extent to which the Liberal government's social reform measures put the Conservative Party on the defensive.

1909/10-33

TARIFF REFORM (1910)

This was even more the case with the unpopular aspect of the tariff reform policy, the fear that it would raise the cost of living for working-class families.

1909/10-37

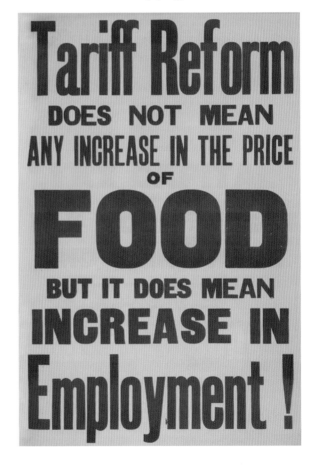

Tariff Reform
DOES NOT MEAN
ANY INCREASE IN THE PRICE
OF
FOOD
BUT IT DOES MEAN
INCREASE IN
Employment !

THE BALDWIN YEARS

The First World War restored the position of the Conservative Party as the patriotic party committed to the fullest prosecution of the war effort. It returned to office when Asquith was forced by crises in the management of the war to create a coalition government in May 1915, and took a much greater share of power when its leaders supported Lloyd George's ousting of Asquith as prime minister in December 1916. The latter event badly divided the Liberal Party, and played a major part in its rapid decline in the years immediately following the war. At the end of the conflict, the Conservative leaders decided to continue in the coalition under Lloyd George's leadership, as there would be many difficulties to cope with in the unsettled post-war world. One cause of their uncertainty was the enormous increase in the number of voters due to the Reform Act of 1918, which essentially created a democratic electorate. In 1918, the franchise was given to men at age 21 and women at age 30; a decade later, in 1928, this was equalised for both sexes at age 21. There was also concern about the advance of Communist revolution in Russia and central Europe, and the rise of the Labour Party at home. In the early 1920s, the latter replaced the dwindling Liberal Party as the main left-of-centre alternative to the Conservatives, becoming the official opposition in 1922.

In October 1922, a revolt from below within the Conservative Party overthrew the discredited and unpopular coalition, ejecting not only Lloyd George but also most of the Conservative leaders. The former leader of the party from Balfour's resignation in 1911 to 1921, Andrew Bonar Law, took office as prime minister and called an immediate election, at which the Conservatives unexpectedly won an overall majority. However, terminal illness forced him to resign after only six months in office, and in May 1923 he was succeeded by the relatively inexperienced Stanley Baldwin. A few

THE SOCIALIST IDOL

OFFICIALDOM

STATE CONTROL

DON'T FEED THE IDOL–SMASH IT!

VOTE CONSERVATIVE

months later, faced with rising unemployment and the advance of the Labour Party, Baldwin concluded that the only remedy was to introduce protection. However, after he announced this conviction at the Conservative Party annual conference in October 1923, the situation slipped rapidly out of control and he was forced to call a general election for December. Once again, tariff reform proved to be an electoral liability: the policy succeeded in reuniting the bitterly divided Liberal Party, dismayed many Conservatives, and again raised fears about the increased cost of staple foodstuffs. The Conservatives fell from 344 seats in 1922 to 258 in 1923; although they remained the largest single party in the House of Commons, they had clearly been rejected by the electorate and were outnumbered by the combined strength of the two free-trade parties, Labour returning 191 MPs and the Liberals 158. The consequence, after the Christmas recess, was the installation of the first minority Labour government in January 1924, with Ramsay MacDonald becoming prime minister.

This government had some successes during its eight months in office, and the general election which followed in October 1924 did far greater damage to the Liberals than it did to Labour. Baldwin had dropped the protectionist policy in favour of a moderate reformist programme, and, together with his attractive and conciliatory public image, this led to a Conservative landslide: the party won 412 seats, whilst Labour dropped back to 151 and the Liberals crashed disastrously to a mere 40. Baldwin's second government of 1924–29 introduced a wide range of social reforms, including pensions for widows and orphans in 1925 and substantial measures on housing, welfare provision, local government and the rating system. Following the defeat of the General Strike of 1926, it amended the laws relating to trade unions in 1927, in the face of sustained Labour opposition. The government lasted for a normal term, and when Baldwin called the general election in May 1929 it was the most normal of all those in the inter-war period, coming at the expected time and without any crises or coalition pacts. The major issue was unemployment, which the government had been unable to reduce below a level of around one million; indeed, the return to the gold standard in 1925 had made matters worse by overpricing British goods in the world markets.

The general election of 1929 was a high point in the use and design of political posters. They were a key weapon of political propaganda, and the Conservatives used 464,000 during the campaign. There had been plenty of time to prepare; as well as expanding its publicity department, Central Office consulted a leading advertising agency of the day, S.H. Benson. A wide range of colourful and stylishly designed posters were produced, some warning of the dangers of socialism and others extolling the record of the Conservative government. The main positive proposal was a cautious extension of 'safeguarding', which was a restricted form of tariff protection for industries with specific problems; any form of 'food taxes' was explicitly ruled out. Baldwin was widely recognised to be the party's greatest electoral asset, and the theme of 'Trust Baldwin' was a cornerstone of the campaign. Bensons built on this with the suggestion of echoing a current road safety campaign by adopting the slogan 'Safety First', but this became a focus of criticism when the outcome was a defeat. As had been feared, the attempt of Lloyd George to revive the Liberal Party led to a substantial increase in the number of three-way contests and consequently the loss of many of the marginal seats won in 1924. The Conservatives fell back to 260 seats, but the Liberals advanced only slightly to 59; the real gainer was the Labour Party, which with 287 seats became for the first time the largest party in the House of Commons, and MacDonald formed his second minority administration.

THE TWO FACES OF LLOYD GEORGE (1923)

The poster refers to the fact that the economy of the United States was protected by tariff duties, which Lloyd George and the Liberal Party strongly opposed in Britain.

1923-01

SAFETY FIRST! (1929)

This became the main Conservative slogan in the general election of May 1929, and came in for much criticism after the defeat.

1929-09

TRUST BALDWIN (1929)

This is one of several posters which built on the popularity of Conservative Party leader Stanley Baldwin and his image as an honest and plain man.

1929-32

This references Baldwin's habit of pipe-smoking (later deliberately echoed by Labour prime minister Harold Wilson); in this period, smoking was widespread and there was no awareness of the health risk, so this image was without negative connotations.

1929-44

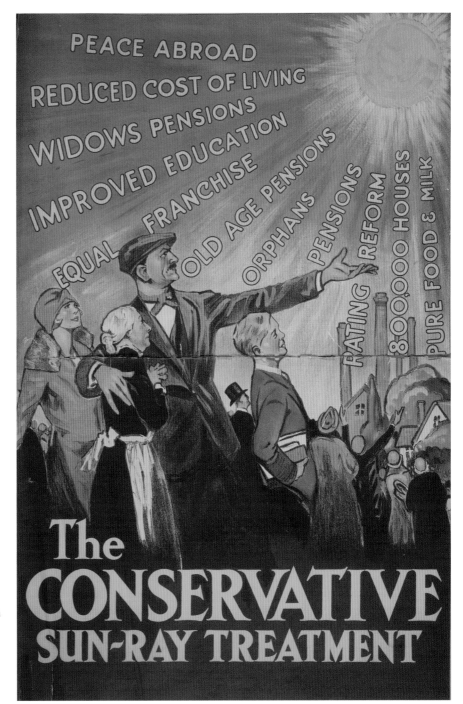

THE CONSERVATIVE SUN-RAY TREATMENT (1929)

This poster trumpets the social reform record of the 1924–29 Conservative government, which was seen as essential in the first general election to be held with full adult suffrage for men and women aged over 21.

1929-24

THE ESCALATOR TO PROSPERITY (1929)

The poster is careful to include figures representative of all classes and both genders.

1929-30

**CONSERVATIVES ARE
INCREASING EMPLOYMENT
(1929)**

Unemployment was a central
issue in the general election, and
played an important part in the
victory of the Labour Party.

1929-36

SAFEGUARDING SHIELDS YOUR WAGES & YOUR JOB!

WORKERS!

VOTE CONSERVATIVE!

SAFEGUARDING SHIELDS YOUR WAGES AND YOUR JOB! (1929)

The striking design of the poster echoes similar poster art in Germany and Soviet Russia; 'safeguarding' was a limited policy of industrial protection which the Conservative manifesto proposed moderately to extend – but with duties on food or raw materials explicitly ruled out.

1929-34

'SAFEGUARDING' IS THE
'OPEN SESAME' (1929)

1929-25

WHAT DO THE TEA-LEAVES SAY? (1929)

This refers to the repeal of the Tea Duty by the free-trade chancellor of the exchequer in the 1924–29 Conservative government, Winston Churchill.

1929-46

STOP THIS (1929)

With the rise of the Labour Party in the 1920s, attacks on the dangers of socialism were a main theme of Conservative propaganda, summed up in this simple but effective image of the national flag being turned into the revolutionary red flag.

1929-45

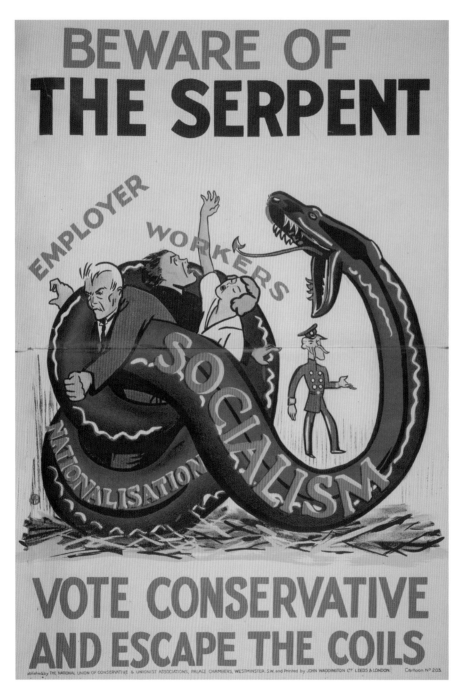

BEWARE OF THE SERPENT (1929)

Socialism is depicted as crushing not only the capitalist but also the workers who depend upon him for employment; the figure seen in profile below the serpent's head, wearing a strange version of a Soviet-style commissar's uniform, is the leader of the Labour Party, Ramsay MacDonald.

1929-26

SOCIALISM WOULD MEAN INSPECTORS ALL ROUND (1929)

This poster plays on the fact that the interference of government regulators, who in the nineteenth century were often imposing middle-class values and morality, was unpopular with the public. The uniformed and hostile state officials are shown here literally sticking their noses into the Englishman's home, with an implicit reference to the popular attitude that 'an Englishman's home is his castle'.

1929-31

39

THE SOCIALIST IDOL (1929)

1929-38

FREE INDUSTRY FROM
THE RED BAR OF SOCIALISM!
(1929)

1929-42

ANOTHER LEG-UP FROM THE LIBERALS! (1929)

This warns of the danger from Lloyd George's revival of the Liberal Party in 1927–29, and refers back to the role played by the Liberals when Labour formed its first minority government in 1924. In the 1929 general election, the increased number of Liberal candidates and the resulting three-cornered contests were a major cause of the Conservative defeat, and after the election the Labour Party took office for the second time, again without an overall majority in the House of Commons. In the poster, the Labour leader, Ramsay MacDonald, is shown as standing on Lloyd George's back.

1929-29

SO PRETTY! –
'TILL THEY BURST! (1929)

A theme of the Conservative
campaign was the irresponsible
promises of the opposition
parties, which were contrasted
with Baldwin's more cautious
but more honest message;
the Labour leader, Ramsay
MacDonald, is on the left,
and the Liberal leader, Lloyd
George, is on the right.

1929-28

NATIONAL CRISIS AND THE NATIONAL GOVERNMENTS

The Great Depression began with the collapse of the American stock market in the autumn of 1929, and the following worldwide recession had a devastating impact on the British economy in 1930 and 1931, with the value of Britain's export trade falling by nearly half. Since taking office in June 1929, the second Labour government had disappointed its supporters and demonstrated that it lacked effective policies with which to tackle unemployment, despite its election claim that as the party of the working class it had a special understanding of the problem. Unemployment had stood at 1.2 million when MacDonald became prime minister; by June 1930 it had risen to 1.9 million, and in January 1931 it reached an unprecedented 2.7 million. Despite an increase in the rate of income tax, the government's spending – including the heavy cost of unemployment benefit – had resulted in a widening budget deficit, which by the summer of 1931 was causing increasing concern in financial markets at home and overseas.

This developing crisis turned critical in early August 1931, due to the exposed position of sterling following a banking collapse in central Europe and the revelation that the deficit would be much larger than expected. Over the next three weeks, as the economic situation worsened and projections of the deficit grew even higher, the Labour cabinet wrangled over various possible ways of balancing the budget, but were divided over the need to cut unemployment benefit. However, without this, the reduction in spending was too little to restore overseas confidence, and withdrawals of gold reserves from the Bank of England reached a critical level. The Labour cabinet finally broke up on 23 August, with MacDonald intending to resign as prime minister, and on the next day the leaders of the three parties met at Buckingham Palace. Partly under pressure from King George V, and partly due to the atmosphere of panic and urgency which dominated the crisis, they agreed to form a

temporary 'National Government' to balance the budget, save the pound and maintain the gold standard. MacDonald remained as prime minister, and Philip Snowden, the chancellor of the exchequer, and two other members of the Labour ministry joined the emergency cabinet of ten, together with four Conservatives and two Liberals. This was not an outcome that the Conservatives had wanted, for by the summer of 1931 they had seemed on course for an election victory on the scale of 1924. Under the impact of the slump, public confidence in free trade was disappearing, and for the first time a protectionist programme would be a vote winner not just in the depressed agricultural counties but also in the urban industrial districts. However, the need for national unity to restore overseas confidence in Britain took priority, and as the patriotic party the Conservatives could not refuse this duty.

The National Government passed a package of measures to balance the budget, but the pressure on the pound increased and on 21 September the gold standard had to be abandoned. Almost all of the Labour Party had gone into opposition, bitterly denouncing the new ministry and their former leader, and it became essential, if overseas and domestic confidence was to be restored, for the government to stay together and to demonstrate that it had popular support. However, the cabinet nearly broke up over the issue of free trade versus tariffs, until an agreement was reached on 5 October that the government as a whole would only ask for an undefined 'doctor's mandate' to take whatever measures it considered necessary, and its component parties would campaign on their own policies. This was a crucial requirement for the Conservatives, who provided most of the MPs and candidates, and who were determined to secure an endorsement of their protectionist programme. Parliament was dissolved on the next day, and the outcome of the poll on 27 October was the biggest landslide in British history. The Labour Party retained only 52 seats, whilst the National Government as a whole returned 558 MPs, of whom 470 were Conservatives. Most of the posters for this campaign were appeals for general support of the National Government, but those which related to the specific issues of unrestricted imports under free trade, protection for agriculture or preference for the Empire appeared with the party's name, either alone or in conjunction with the National appeal.

Following the Imperial Conference at Ottawa in the summer of 1932, protectionist measures were introduced which included preference for Empire goods. This abandonment of free trade caused the departure of Snowden and about half of the Liberal Party, led by Sir Herbert Samuel. However, the other half of the Liberal Party remained, and the continued presence of MacDonald as prime minister until June 1935, and of a significant number of 'National Labour' and 'National Liberal' cabinet ministers, meant that the government retained credibility as a broad-based coalition with a wide appeal. It was not a barely disguised Conservative front, and followed policies which were cross-party in content and spirit, particularly with interventionist measures on agriculture and housing in domestic policy, support for disarmament and the League of Nations in foreign policy, and reforms of imperial government in India – the latter vigorously opposed by Winston Churchill and a minority of 'diehard' right-wing Conservative MPs.

Unemployment peaked at nearly 3 million in the winter of 1932–33, but after this there were signs of a slow but definite improvement. Although some of the older industrial areas remained unemployment 'black spots', in other parts of the country the development of new industries such as vehicle manufacture, light engineering and electrical goods was bringing a return to prosperity. By the autumn of 1935, the National Government could confidently and credibly present a record of having steered the country to better times. There was no Conservative opposition to continuing the National combination, as there were no conflicts of principle dividing its component parts and the benefits of continuing it were self-evident. The Conservative Party leader, Baldwin, succeeded MacDonald as prime minister in June 1935 and called a general election in November, which was a comfortable victory. With 429 MPs (of whom 387 were Conservatives), the National Government retained a large majority over Labour, who recovered some ground with 154 MPs, whilst Samuel's independent Liberals were reduced to 21 seats. The election turned mainly on domestic issues, but international tensions with the European dictatorships led to emphasis upon the National Government's commitment to peace, whilst at the same time Baldwin sought a mandate for moderate defensive rearmament, particularly against the threat of attack from the air.

SMOKELESS CHIMNEYS AND ANXIOUS MOTHERS! (1931)

The design of this poster echoes the famous recruiting poster of the early First World War, 'Women Of Britain Say Go!', although the family now appear in distress rather than exhibiting patriotic pride.

1931-04

STOP THIS (1931)

The poster refers to the free-trade system of unrestricted imports of foreign goods as a main cause of unemployment in Britain. As with other posters promoting the specifically Conservative policy of protectionism, it uses the name of the party rather than of the National Government as a whole.

1931-12

48

IT'S YOUR MONEY! (1931)

This refers to the spending levels of the previous Labour government as a cause of the financial crisis of August 1931.

1931-22

49

UNITY AND SECURITY (1931)

The emblematic figure of John Bull, depicted as healthy and prosperous, parachutes from the failed vehicle of socialism to a safe landing, thanks to the National Government.

1931-05

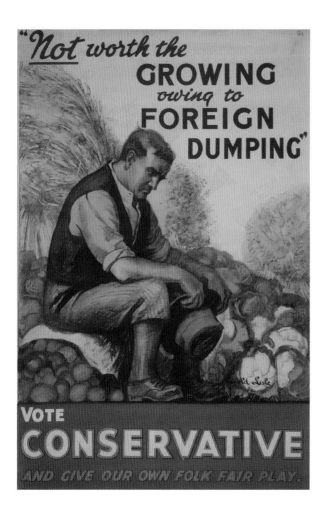

NOT WORTH THE GROWING (1931)

The Conservative policy of protectionism was most popular in the depressed agricultural sector; 'foreign dumping' was the term for the competition from imports which had benefited from a subsidy or were surplus produce being sold at below cost price.

1931-21

BACK TO THE PLOUGH (1931)

1931-17

THE DAWN OF BRIGHTER DAYS (1931)

The advent of protection is depicted as bringing prosperity back to the countryside.

1931-15

A UNITED EMPIRE! (1931)

This poster refers back to the serious divisions in the Conservative Party when in opposition in 1929–31, during which a United Empire Party was founded to campaign for tariffs and imperial preference; the strife was only ended when the Conservative leadership adopted a 'free hand' policy to introduce tariffs, including food taxes.

1931-06

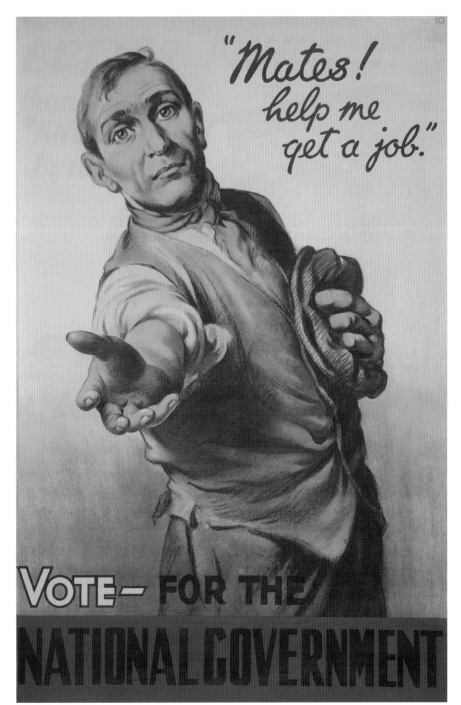

MATES! HELP ME GET A JOB (1931)

This poster became an iconic image of the 1931 campaign; like the famous 'Lord Kitchener' recruiting poster of 1914, the eyes and hand of the figure seem to follow the observer, whatever the angle of view.

1931-10

53

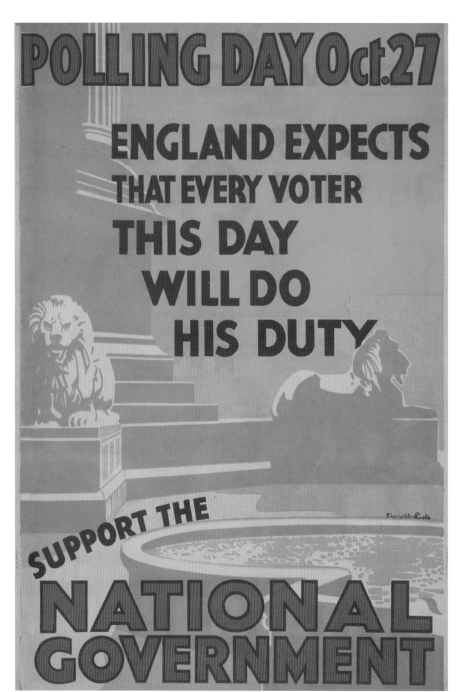

ENGLAND EXPECTS (1931)

The atmosphere of national crisis and the call to patriotic duty were evoked by this echo of Nelson's famous signal at the Battle of Trafalgar (which would have been familiar to every citizen), reinforced by the background image of the lions and the base of Nelson's memorial column in Trafalgar Square, London.

1931–20

**JOIN THIS MARCH TO
PROSPERITY AND PEACE
(1935)**

These were the twin themes
of the National Government's
appeal for re-election in 1935;
the figures in the poster
represent a varied range of men
and women of different classes
and ages.

1935-07

BRITAIN LEADS THE WORLD AGAIN IN EXPORT TRADE (1935)

One of the many posters driving home the message that the National Government had steered the country to better times since the economic crisis of 1931.

1935-05

I GOT THE JOB –
HELP ME TO KEEP IT (1935)

The poster reproduces the
famous image from 1931, with
the working man now neat and
prosperous, and points out the
danger to employment should
the Labour Party be elected.

1935-26

DADDY'S GOT A JOB! (1935)

1935-08

GOOD MONEY (1935)

1935-13

FOR SECURITY AND BETTER
TIMES ON THE LAND (1935)

1935–03

STACKS OF WORK (1935)

1935-04

**FOR PEACE –
BETWEEN NATIONS,
BETWEEN CLASSES (1935)**

This iconic image summarised
the appeal of both the domestic
and the foreign policies of the
National Government.

1935-01

**IT'S TEAM WORK
THAT COUNTS (1935)**

The poster refers to the
cooperation of different parties
in the National Government,
which gave it a wider appeal
than a purely Conservative
administration.

1935-24

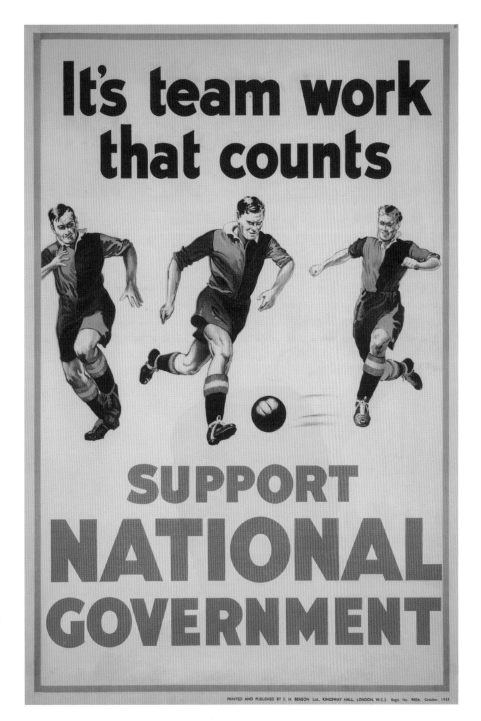

for SECURITY & PEACE WITH SOCIAL IMPROVEMENT Vote NATIONAL

SECURITY & PEACE (1935)

Issues of foreign policy were important in the 1935 general election, with strong public support for the League of Nations and rising concern over the intentions of the fascist dictatorships in Germany and Italy.

1935-21

**KEEP THAT SHADOW
FROM THEM (1935)**

The greatest public fear in a
future war was of devastating
bombing attacks on the civilian
population, and in the 1935
campaign the prime minister,
Stanley Baldwin, sought a
mandate for limited rearmament
which would focus mainly on an
expansion of Britain's air force.

1935-23

OUR WORD IS OUR BOND
(1935)

This poster reinforced the commitment of Britain to the Covenant of the League of Nations.

1935-17

CHURCHILL'S PEACETIME LEADERSHIP

The Conservative Party suffered its second major defeat of the twentieth century in 1945, at the end of the Second World War. Several factors contributed to this, of which the most important was a shift in public attitudes in the period between the Dunkirk evacuation in June 1940 and the victory at El Alamein in November 1942. During this period, a retrospective view became deeply entrenched which held the National Governments to blame for the perceived failures of the 1930s: not only the lack of rearmament and the appeasement of the dictators, but also the human waste of unemployment during the depression and a parsimonious social policy. There was a powerful sentiment of 'never again', and this was paralleled by the demand, also seen in the First World War, that such struggle and sacrifice should lead to a better and fairer post-war society. This was crystallised by the Beveridge Report, which appeared at the turning point of the war in December 1942, and set out proposals for the future 'welfare state' in the provision of a national health service and an integrated social security system. When this was debated in the House of Commons in March 1943, the negativism of Conservative ministers and MPs, concerned about its cost, was in striking contrast to the open approval from the Labour Party, and this left a lasting impression. By the end of 1942, opinion polls indicated that about 40 per cent of the population had changed their political outlook since the start of the war, and this was almost entirely in one direction – towards Labour.

The National Governments of the 1930s had come to an end in May 1940, when defeat in the Norwegian campaign led to the replacement of Neville Chamberlain as prime minister by Winston Churchill, who had been a prominent critic of pre-war foreign and defence policy. Churchill formed a new coalition, which the opposition Liberal and Labour parties

for family - happiness - and a home

VOTE CONSERVATIVE

joined, and which also used the name 'National Government'. During the next five years, Churchill concentrated his attention on the conduct of the war, leaving the Home Front mainly in the hands of the leading Labour ministers and allowing the Conservative Party organisation in the country to decay. When victory in Europe was achieved in May 1945, the Liberal and Labour parties withdrew from the coalition to fight the general election independently. Churchill continued as prime minister of a reduced 'caretaker' government until the election results in July, which unexpectedly ejected him from office. However, whilst personally popular for his war leadership, Churchill was seen by many voters as not the best peacetime leader, and his harsh criticisms of Labour during the election campaign had struck a jarring note. The election left the Conservative Party and its remaining National Liberal allies with 210 seats, the independent Liberal Party with only 12, and the Labour Party with 393, giving it a massive overall majority.

After the immediate shock had passed, this defeat led naturally to reappraisals of both policy and organisation. Churchill continued as party leader, but left much of the detailed work to his deputy and heir apparent, Anthony Eden, and the rising figure of R.A. Butler, who took over the Conservative Research Department. Together with the party chairman, the former businessman Lord Woolton, who raised large funds and revitalised the party organisation, they were determined to look forward rather than back. Eden took up the theme of a 'property-owning democracy' in his speeches, whilst Butler was responsible for the policy statement which endorsed greater state interventionism, *The Industrial Charter* of May 1947. During the Labour governments of 1945–51, the Conservatives were careful in what they opposed in order not to reawaken fears that they were reactionary, and so they accepted the pillars of the post-war 'consensus': the welfare state, the public ownership of certain industries, government intervention to manage the economy on Keynesian principles, and partnership in industry between trade unions and employers. However, there were areas where the government could be attacked, especially the economic difficulties which led to a tightening of wartime rationing after 1947, the devaluation of the pound in 1949 and a relative lack of progress over house building, which was a key issue after the destruction of many homes by bombing.

The austerity measures, the restrictive government controls and bureaucracy, and the endless queues for rations eroded the Labour government's support among the middle classes and housewives of all classes. When a general election was called by the Labour leader Clement Attlee in February 1950, the Conservatives advanced to 298 MPs and Labour fell back to 315; with nine Liberal MPs, this left Labour barely clinging to office with an overall majority of only 8. With many of the Labour leaders ill or exhausted after a decade in office, this proved to be an untenable position, and a further general election followed in October 1951. Two factors were important in its outcome: a popular Conservative pledge to build 300,000 new houses each year and a slump in the number of Liberal candidates compared to the 1950 election, which led to more straight fights with Labour. Fewer seats changed hands than in 1950, but the result tipped the balance to the Conservatives: with 321 seats to Labour's 295 and 9 Liberals, Churchill returned to Downing Street for a second term as prime minister. His ministry deliberately followed a moderate policy, making sure that Labour predictions of the dismantling of the welfare state were proved groundless – indeed, the government positively trumpeted its record of expenditure on the social services and similar reforms. Improvement in the economic situation enabled wartime rationing to be wound down in the early 1950s, and the atmosphere began to change from one of drab austerity to affluence, with rising standards of living.

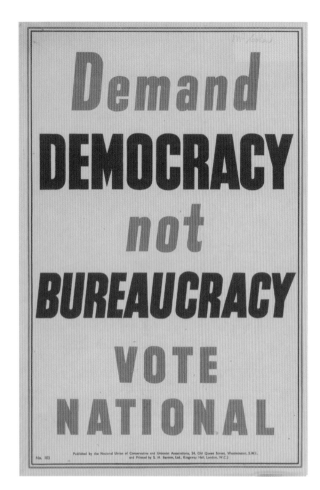

**DEMAND DEMOCRACY
NOT BUREAUCRACY (1945)**

1945-07

It was widely expected that Churchill would sweep to victory in 1945 as the 'man who won the war', as Lloyd George had done in 1918. However, despite public appreciation and gratitude for his wartime role, he was seen by many people as not best suited for a peacetime government of reconstruction and social reform.

1945-12

**AFTER 4 YEARS LABOUR
(1950)**

1950–05

for family -
happiness - and a home

VOTE
CONSERVATIVE

**FOR FAMILY, HAPPINESS,
AND A HOME (1950)**

One of the first Conservative
posters to feature a respectable
'typical' nuclear family, middle
class or prosperous working
class, and to link the message
of family with that of home
ownership.

1950–09

72

THOUGHT FOR TO-DAY (1950)

Against the background of the worsening Cold War, this poster makes the connection between socialism and communism.

1950-11

MAKE BRITAIN GREAT AGAIN (1950)

The bulldog was not only an emblematic symbol of Britain, but also a specific reference to the leader of the Conservative Party, Winston Churchill, both for his jowly facial appearance and for his dogged determination in the dark days of the Second World War. This version of the poster was used in Northern Ireland; the mainland edition differed in having 'Conservative' as the bottom line.

1950–01

A VOTE FOR THE LIBERALS IS A VOTE WASTED (1950)

The role of the Liberal Party was crucial in the outcome of the 1950 and 1951 general elections, with the large reduction in the number of Liberal candidates in 1951 helping the Conservatives to eventual victory.

1950–04

a vote for the LIBERALS LIBERALS is a vote wasted

VOTE CONSERVATIVE
The Right Road for Britain

75

**CUT OUT
GOVERNMENT WASTE
(1951)**

The 1945–51 Labour
government's nationalisation
programme had greatly
extended the role of the state,
and examples of wasteful
spending were highlighted and
attacked by the Conservative
opposition.

1951-04

DON'T THROW A SPANNER IN THE STEELWORKS (1951)

The taking into public ownership of the iron and steel industry was the only Labour nationalisation that the Conservative Party strongly opposed, and that (together with road haulage) they reversed when returning to office after 1951.

1951-15

Don't throw a spanner in the STEELworks

Help the CONSERVATIVES to set steel free

KEEP VOTING CONSERVATIVE (1952)

With a strengthening economy, the Conservative government of 1951–55 was able to end wartime rationing and other restrictions, and to gain the credit for this.

1952-02

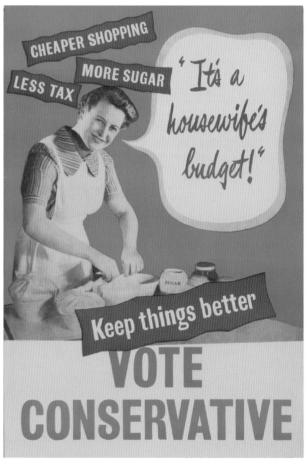

IN 1952 MORE WAS SPENT ON EDUCATION THAN EVER BEFORE (1952)

The government was keen to refute Labour claims that the Conservatives would dismantle the new welfare state, and so posters emphasised the higher level of social expenditure.

1952–04

NEW HOMES FOR A MILLION FOLK LAST YEAR (1954)

An important commitment in the Conservative manifesto in 1951 had been a target of building 300,000 new houses each year, and this poster publicises the achievement of this by 1954.

1954–07

IT'S FULL EMPLOYMENT (1954)

1954-12

SAFEGUARDING PEACE (1954)

1954-16

'NEVER HAD IT SO GOOD' – THE AGE OF AFFLUENCE

Churchill suffered a serious stroke in 1953, but it took until April 1955 to persuade him to retire. After a long wait as heir apparent, Anthony Eden succeeded him as prime minister and immediately called a general election, which took place on 26 May 1955. Eden was a handsome and charismatic figure, and his vigour contrasted effectively with the Labour Party, which had been divided over issues relating to the Cold War and the development of British nuclear weapons. In the pre-election budget in April, the chancellor of the exchequer, R.A. Butler, had lowered taxes (although, due to signs of the economy overheating, some of this embarrassingly had to be reversed later in the year), and real wage levels were rising. The government had achieved its ambitious pledge to build 300,000 new houses a year, and this together with the increased levels of pensions and social security benefits were highlighted in the party's election posters. The outcome was an increased majority, with the Conservatives advancing to 345 seats and Labour slipping back to 277; as in 1951, only 6 Liberal MPs were elected.

go AHEAD go Conservative

This gave Eden a comfortable majority, and at first the prospects looked favourable. However, criticisms of a lack of direction in domestic policy began to be voiced, even before the crisis over the nationalisation of the Suez Canal by the Egyptian regime of Colonel Nasser in July 1956. The government determined to recover the canal by means of a joint military operation with France, but this took some time to prepare and did not take place until the end of October. However, by this time public opinion had cooled and was less willing to support the use of force, and the invasion of the Canal Zone was opposed by the Labour and Liberal parties. More seriously, Eden had ignored warning signals from President Eisenhower, who was running for re-election at this time, and the United States refused to support what seemed to be an exercise in old-fashioned gunboat imperialism. A run on the pound began, and humiliatingly the military operation had to be called off before the necessary financial support could be obtained from the USA. Under the strain, Eden's health – which had been fragile ever since a botched operation in 1953 – gave way. He departed to the Caribbean over Christmas 1956 in an effort to recover, but on his return was told by his doctors that he could not go on.

Harold Macmillan, who had overseen the successful housing drive in 1951–54 and had replaced Butler at the Treasury in December 1955, succeeded Eden as prime minister on 10 January 1957. He faced a difficult situation, with the government's prestige at home and abroad badly damaged by the Suez fiasco. Macmillan moved swiftly to repair relations with the United States, and met with the re-elected Eisenhower at Bermuda in March 1957. The morale of the Conservative Party had been shaken, but Macmillan's show of determination and confidence led to a recovery. He acquired an image of 'unflappability', and was depicted in a famous cartoon of the day as 'Supermac'. The underlying economic situation appeared strong, with unemployment at its lowest level since 1945. This was a period of rising living standards for many families, with spreading ownership of consumer durables such as refrigerators, washing machines, televisions and motor cars. This was the affluence which Macmillan famously referred to in a speech at Bedford in July 1957: 'Let us be frank about it, most of our people have never had it so good.' His remark was intended not as a boast but as a plain statement of fact, and it was the combination of prosperity and full employment which was the basis of victory when Macmillan called a general election in October 1959. It was now the Labour Party which had an unattractive legacy from the past, as the party of rationing, controls and nationalisation, and the Conservatives who emphasised themes of opportunity, freedom and choice, appealing to the aspirations of the key electoral group of the 'young marrieds', men and women aged 25–40. These themes were captured in the iconic poster of this election, with its depiction of such a family and the slogan: 'Life's better with the Conservatives – don't let Labour ruin it'. The result of the election was that the government was not only re-elected, but unprecedentedly increased its majority yet again. The Conservatives gained twenty seats and, with 365 MPs, had a majority of a hundred over the 258 Labour MPs and the 6 Liberals.

Following this victory, some commentators questioned whether the Labour Party could ever win again, due to the shrinking size of its industrial working-class base and the advantages possessed by the government in managing the economy to produce pre-election prosperity. However, the problems and mistakes of the government after 1961 changed the situation, and led to a revival in Labour's fortunes. Long-term economic problems, particularly of wage increases not matched by improved productivity, began to take effect. Growth slowed, visibly lagging behind the six countries of the recently formed European Economic Community, imports increased, and from 1960 onwards the balance of trade steadily worsened. This led to attempts to control prices and incomes, with the 'pay pause' of 1961, and 'stop–go' policies seeking to stimulate the economy. The resultant unpopularity contributed to a revival of the Liberal Party, with a surprise by-election win in stockbroker-belt Orpington in March 1962, and to Macmillan's replacement of one-third of his cabinet in July 1962 – a sweeping reshuffle which was intended to be decisive, but instead looked like panic. Macmillan appeared to be losing his touch and to be out of tune with a changing society, and was especially damaged by his naive mishandling of the Profumo sex-and-spying scandal of 1963. His attempt to join the EEC ended in humiliating failure with the veto of the French president, de Gaulle, in January 1963. Macmillan always favoured expansionist policies, and the 1963 budget of his new chancellor, Reginald Maudling, launched a 'dash for growth' with tax cuts of £300 million. Instead, imports were sucked in, government borrowing increased, and the budget deficit reached record levels. Macmillan was contemplating announcing that he would not lead the party into the next election when a sudden admission to hospital in October 1963, on the eve of the party's annual conference, led him to resign immediately.

WORKING FOR PEACE

WORKING FOR PEACE (1955)

This general election poster
features the new Conservative
leader and prime minister,
Sir Anthony Eden, who
had previously been foreign
secretary.

1955-03

**QUEUES, CONTROLS,
RATIONING (1955)**

The poster refers back to the
shortages and rationing of the
austerity period during the
previous Labour government in
1945–51.

1955-04

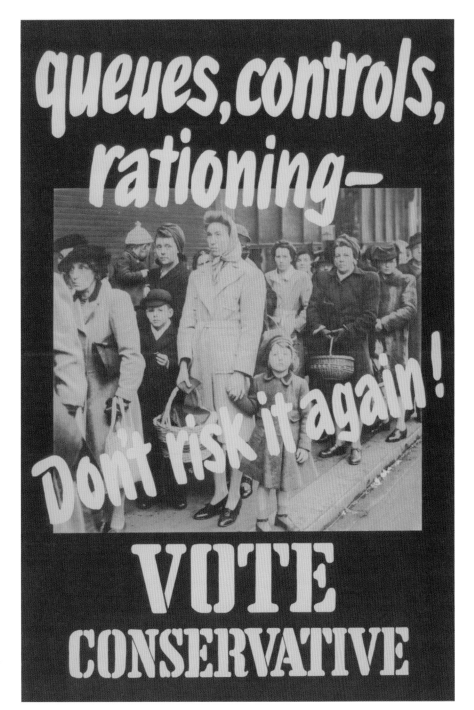

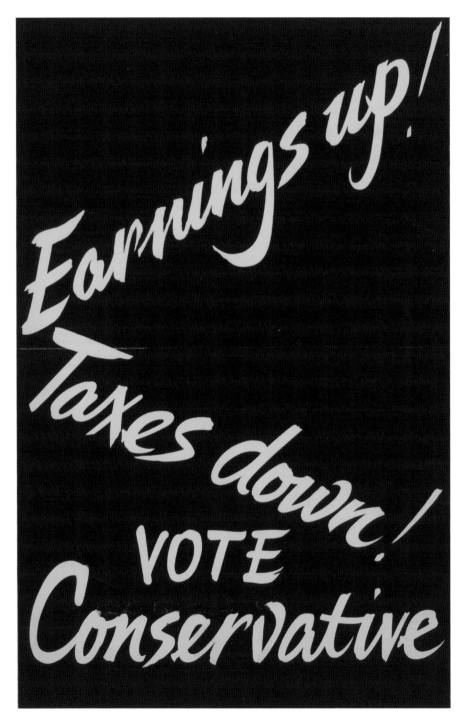

EARNINGS UP! TAXES DOWN! (1955)

This refers not only to the general rise in living standards, but also to the tax reductions in the pre-election budget of April 1955.

1955-01

**PENSIONS – BENEFITS –
BEST EVER! (1955)**

One of several posters
emphasising that the welfare
state had prospered under the
Conservative government of
1951–55.

1955-07

CF 106   Published by the Conservative & Unionist Central Office, Abbey House, 2-8 Victoria Street, S.W.1 and printed by Hypnocolor Ltd. (T.U.), London

SHOUT IT FROM A MILLION
NEW HOUSETOPS (1955)

1955-14

PRODUCE MORE, EARN MORE,
SAVE MORE (1955)

1955-15

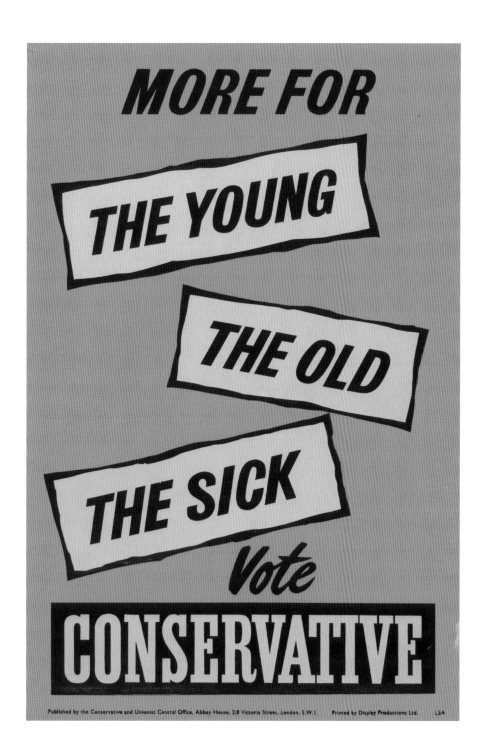

MORE FOR THE YOUNG,
THE OLD, THE SICK (1955)

1955-19

KEEP YOUR
GRAMMAR SCHOOL (1956)

From the mid-1950s, the issue of comprehensive education versus the retention of grammar schools became a significant political issue.

1956-04

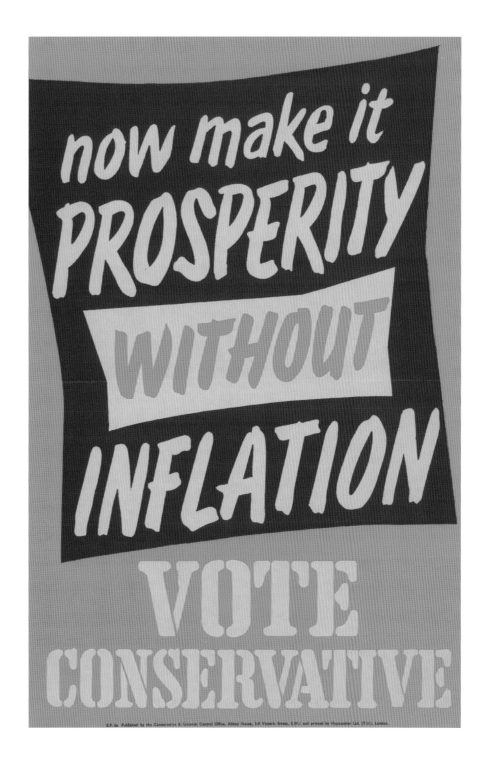

**PROSPERITY WITHOUT
INFLATION (1956)**

1956–05

LEADING BRITAIN (1958)

The poster features Harold
Macmillan, leader of the
Conservative Party and prime
minister since January 1957, who
at this time was at the height of
his popularity.

1958-03

B.B.C or I.T.V programme?

You've a choice –
thanks to the Conservatives...

because

CONSERVATIVES BELIEVE IN OPPORTUNITY

**BBC OR ITV PROGRAMME?
(1958)**

With the growth of television ownership, the Conservative government had authorised the start of independent broadcasting, in competition with the BBC, so there were now two television channels for viewers to watch. Here this is linked to the broader and perennial Conservative themes of choice and opportunity.

1958-01

TRUST THE PARTY THAT TRUSTS LOCAL GOVERNMENT!
(1958)

This poster, produced for use in local elections, emphasises the considerable Conservative participation and interest in local government.

1958-11

YOU'RE HAVING IT GOOD (1959)

This general election poster refers back to Macmillan's famous remark about the rise in affluence, that 'most of our people have never had it so good', which was originally made in a speech at Bedford in July 1957.

1959-15

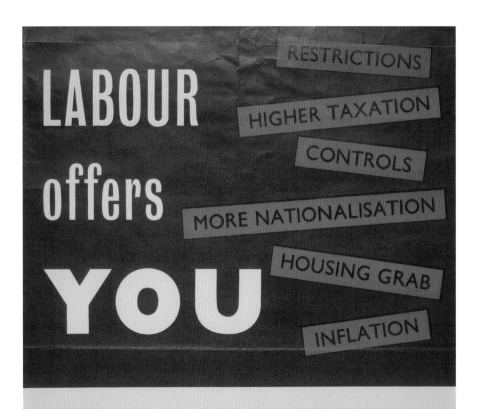

LABOUR OFFERS YOU (1959)

1959-01

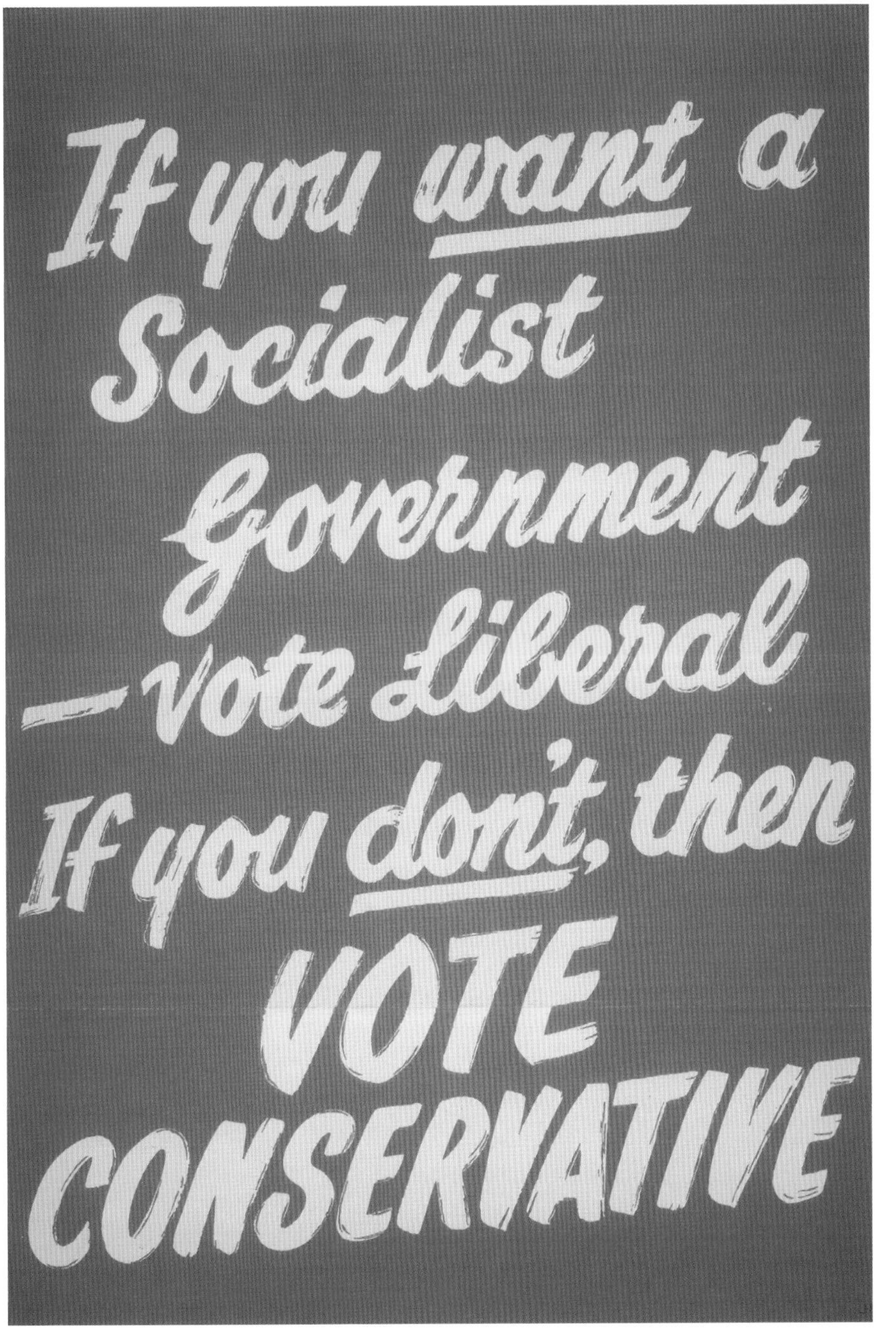

**IF YOU WANT A
SOCIALIST GOVERNMENT –
VOTE LIBERAL (1959)**

The start of a modest Liberal
revival in the late 1950s was
a cause for concern for the
Conservatives, as elections
with larger numbers of Liberal
candidates standing had
previously led to their defeat.

1959–03

LIFE'S BETTER
WITH THE CONSERVATIVES
(1959)

This depiction of a typical affluent family, with the tag line of 'Don't let Labour ruin it', was the iconic summary of the Conservative message – both positive and negative – in the 1959 general election; note the new television set in the background.

1959-02

For more **schools** and better **schools**

VOTE CONSERVATIVE

Era PUBLISHED BY THE CONSERVATIVE & UNIONIST CENTRAL OFFICE, 32 SMITH SQUARE, S.W.1, AND PRINTED BY TAYLOR GARNETT EVANS & CO. LTD, WATFORD, HERTS.

**FOR MORE SCHOOLS
AND BETTER SCHOOLS (1959)**

1959-26

CLUBMEN! (1960)

This poster for use in the local elections was particularly aimed at the large number of members of Conservative Clubs across the country, many of whom were notoriously hard to mobilise for political activity.

1960–04

**THINK OF THE FUTURE
(1960–61)**

The Young Conservatives
movement was very popular
in the period from the late
1940s to the mid-1960s, with
a large membership attracted
particularly by the social
opportunities that it provided.

1960/1–03

MORE SCHOOLS,
BETTER SCHOOLS,
WIDER EDUCATIONAL
OPPORTUNITIES (1961)

1961-03

GO AHEAD (1962)

1962–06

£2 MILLION A WEEK FOR NEW ROADS (1963)

This poster refers to the start of the construction of motorways in Britain, and specifically to the increased public spending in Maudling's 'dash for growth' budget of 1963.

1963-03

TEST BAN TREATY (1963)

The poster shows the symbol of the unilateralist Campaign for Nuclear Disarmament, with the suggestion that the young man is one of the marchers in its annual demonstration at the nuclear weapons research centre at Aldermaston, and it contrasts this with Macmillan's foreign policy success in promoting the Nuclear Test Ban Treaty, a significant step towards multilateral disarmament and détente in the Cold War.

1963-04

...meanwhile the Conservatives have signed the Test Ban Treaty.

SEARCHING FOR A ROLE

Macmillan's unexpected departure left the Conservative Party in disarray, and the competition to succeed him was played out in the full glare of publicity at the party conference. Macmillan sought to orchestrate matters from his hospital bed, with the aim of ensuring that R.A. Butler was not chosen. In this he was successful, but the selection of the foreign secretary, the 14th Earl of Home, caused other problems. Two of the rising young figures in the cabinet, Enoch Powell and Iain Macleod, refused to serve under Home, and Macleod published a damaging attack on the secretive 'magic circle' methods by which the new prime minister had been chosen. More importantly, although he had once been an MP, Home had inherited the earldom in 1951 and was currently a member of the House of Lords. He took advantage of recently passed legislation which allowed him to repudiate his peerage, and a by-election vacancy was quickly arranged for a Scottish seat, so that within a few weeks he had re-entered the House of Commons. Nevertheless, Home's aristocratic background perpetuated the 'grouse moor' image of the Conservative Party as outdated, hidebound and class-conscious. It was now the Labour Party which appeared to be modern and meritocratic; its new leader, Harold Wilson, was adroit in projecting a classless tone and in aligning himself with scientific innovation and managerial efficiency. Home was not a good performer on the increasingly vital medium of television, whereas Wilson was comfortable and urbane. Sir Alec Douglas-Home, as the new leader had become, postponed the election to the very end of the five-year parliament, hoping (as did later prime ministers in 1997 and 2010) that the economic situation would improve. It did not, and Labour's attack focused on the state of the country, attacking the Conservative record as having been '13 wasted years'. When the election finally took place in October 1964, the Conservatives lost power. However,

their 100-seat majority was a huge barrier to overcome, and the result left
Labour ahead only by the tiny majority of 4: there were 317 Labour MPs to
304 Conservatives and 9 Liberals.

This was clearly an unstable situation, and another election would be
inevitable before long. At first, when it seemed this might be imminent,
Douglas-Home stayed on as leader, but restiveness grew due to his lack
of impact in the House of Commons and with the public. In August 1965,
after presiding over the introduction of a formal system to elect future
Conservative leaders by a secret ballot of MPs, he decided to stand down.
In the following contest, Edward Heath beat Reginald Maudling by 150
votes to 133, with 15 MPs voting for Powell. Heath was regarded as forceful
and administratively able, although not a great orator, and his lower-middle-
class background was thought more publicly acceptable than the aristocratic
image of Macmillan and Douglas-Home. In March 1966, Wilson dissolved
parliament and secured a comfortable Labour win; the Conservatives lost
over 50 seats and ended up with only 253, whilst Labour had 364 and
there were now 12 Liberals. The Conservative manifesto for the election
was titled 'Action not Words', a theme intended to emphasise Heath's
plain-speaking purposefulness, and the slogan was repeated in the party's
election posters. These highlighted both traditional Conservative themes,
portraying the ideal middle-class young family, but also new issues which
were to dominate the next decades: the problem of inflation, the role of
the trade unions, and membership of the European Economic Community.
Heath had been the principal negotiator for the Macmillan government's
application to the EEC, and remained firmly committed to securing British
entry.

As he had only recently become party leader, and the defeat was to
a large extent attributed to the problems of the preceding Conservative
government, Heath survived the setback without being challenged. During
the next four years he presided over a major exercise in policy formulation,
although in certain crucial economic areas the difficult questions were
not effectively addressed. Heath was not an inspiring speaker and often
appeared stiff and wooden on television, but his determined efforts won
the respect of his front-bench colleagues and much of the public. Indeed,

as Wilson acquired an image of lack of principle, inconsistency and even deviousness, Heath's rigid course seemed more trustworthy. The Labour government passed a range of important measures on social policy and moral issues, such as race relations, abortion, divorce, the decriminalisation of homosexuality and the suspension of the death penalty. However, once again it was its failures in the economic sphere which correspondingly raised the fortunes of the opposition. The 1966–70 period was marked by increasing disruption from strikes, many of them 'wildcat' or unofficial. The cause of this was the vicious circle of a rising cost of living, leading to wage demands which were not matched by increases in productivity or efficiency, and so their costs were passed on to the consumer as higher prices. The result was inflation and uncompetitive exports, leading to a balance-of-payments deficit, the weakening of the pound, a sterling crisis and, ultimately, a forced devaluation in November 1967. Another setback for the government was the failure of its application to join the EEC, which in the same month met a second veto from de Gaulle. Even so, there seemed to be some improvement, and a favourable by-election result in the spring of 1970 led Wilson to call a general election in June. Unexpectedly poor monthly trade figures announced during the campaign helped the Conservatives, but even so most of the opinion polls, commentators and politicians (including many leading Conservatives) expected Labour to retain power. Only Heath was unshakeably certain of a Conservative victory, and when this was achieved with a very substantial turnover in seats his prestige was greatly enhanced. The Conservative campaign was well targeted on the government's vulnerabilities: the overall campaign slogan offered 'a better tomorrow', but the lasting image was the wastepaper basket filled with Labour's broken promises. The Conservative Party gained nearly 80 seats, with 330 MPs to Labour's 288, whilst the Liberals fell back to only 6 once again.

Vote **CONSERVATIVE**

SIR ALEC DOUGLAS-HOME (1964)

The former 14th Earl of Home succeeded Macmillan as Conservative Party leader and prime minister in October 1963, and led the party in the general election of October 1964.

1964-02

BETTER YOUR STANDARD OF LIVING! (1964)

This poster features another 'ideal family' image, although in this case with three children rather than the usual two.

1964-04

**WARNING - LIBERAL
LETS IN LABOUR (1964)**

Further Liberal advance since
the Orpington by-election of
1962 caused concern in the
marginal constituencies; the
'L-plates' of learner drivers
featured in the design are a
reminder of the inexperience
of the opposition parties in
contrast to the Conservatives,
who had been in office
continuously since 1951.

1964-12

DOWN WITH STATE CONTROL
(1964)

1964-13

NOW WE KNOW HOW LABOUR GOVERNMENT WORKS (1965)

Labour returned to power after the 1964 election, but with a tiny overall majority; this poster was prepared for a likely general election in 1965, although in fact it did not occur until March 1966.

1965-04

C.F.165A   Published by the Conservative & Unionist Central Office, Abbey House, 2/8, Victoria Street, S.W.I.   Printed by Hypnocolor Limited (T.U.) London, E.C.4.

**EQUAL SHARES OF
LESS AND LESS (1965)**

1965–06

ACTION NOT WORDS (1966)

This was the title of the
Conservative manifesto for the
1966 general election, and for
the first time such a slogan was
repeated as a tag line across the
range of the party's posters; this
one features Edward Heath, who
became party leader in August
1965.

1966-05

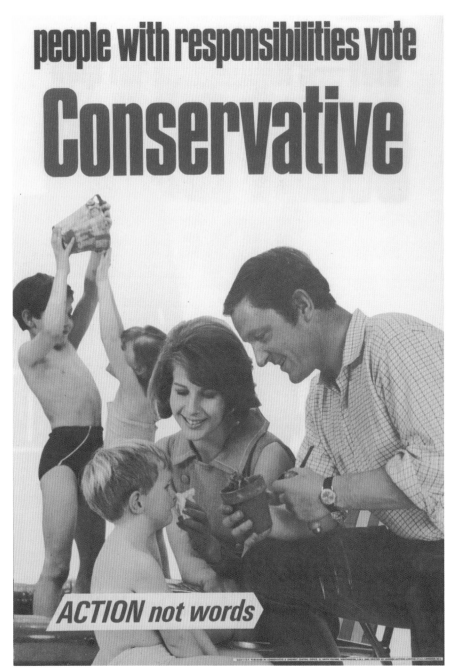

PEOPLE WITH RESPONSIBILITIES (1966)

The 25–40 age range, known as the 'young marrieds', were considered a key electoral demographic group in this period, and this is another poster designed to appeal to them by featuring an aspirational image of an ideal middle-class family.

1966-06

FOR RESPONSIBLE
TRADE UNIONS (1966)

With the economy in decline
and strikes on the increase,
the issue of the role and power
of the trade unions became
a significant issue from the
mid-1960s.

1966-10

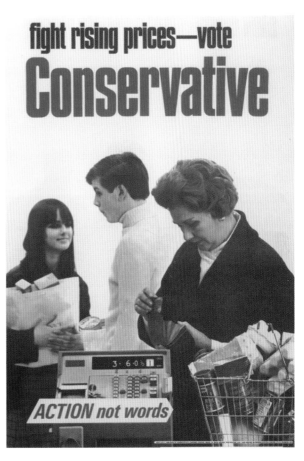

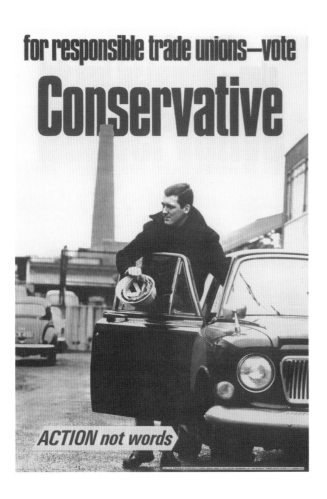

FIGHT RISING PRICES (1966)

Rising prices and inflation
were the other emerging public
concerns in the later 1960s.

1966-14A

with Heath into Europe—vote
Conservative

ACTION not words

WITH HEATH INTO EUROPE (1966)

The Conservative leader was strongly committed to entry into the European Economic Community, having been chief negotiator of the unsuccessful first attempt to join by the Macmillan government; Heath was later to gain entry on the third attempt in 1971.

1966-13

118

**FOR A BETTER TOMORROW
(1970)**

This was the slogan for the 1970 general election, and again was repeated across the campaign; this poster features the party leader, Edward Heath, who was fighting his second general election.

1970–02

For a better tomorrow
vote Conservative

GEP/1/CF Published by Conservative Central Office, 32, Smith Square, London, S.W.1. and Printed by Impress (Acton) Ltd. (T.U.). London. W 3.

Remember Labour's broken promises

For a better tomorrow vote Conservative

REMEMBER LABOUR'S BROKEN PROMISES (1970)

This image of an overflowing wastepaper basket was very effective, and became the most memorable image of the Conservative campaign; it was reinforced by other posters attacking specific aspects of the Labour government's record.

1970–03

The £ in your pocket is now worth

15'7

For a better tomorrow vote Conservative

THE £ IN YOUR POCKET (1970)

This poster focuses on the key issue of inflation, and its wording is a deliberate reference to the controversial broadcast made by Labour prime minister Harold Wilson, after the devaluation of the pound in 1967, in which he stated that this did not mean that 'the pound in your pocket' was now worth less than before.

1970-12

THE 1970s CRISIS

Although it took office with confidence, the Heath government of 1970–74 became a troubled and traumatic period for the Conservative Party. The government struggled to cope with high inflation and rising unemployment, circumstances which were not supposed to occur together according to Keynesian economic theory. Attempts to deal with this situation, especially when unemployment reached 1 million, led to a number of changes in policy. These pragmatic responses included the interventionist Industry Act of 1972, the expansionist budget of the same year, and the introduction of a prices and incomes policy – the very thing for which Labour had been criticised before the election. These 'U-turns' discredited the government's reputation, not only at the time but even more in the reaction that followed in the Thatcher era. Heath had a significant success in negotiating Britain's entry into the European Economic Community, but even this brought problems: the terms were costly (which gave Wilson a pretext for opposing them), and the uncompetitiveness of British industries meant that when entry took effect in January 1973 it added to the economic problems as much as it ameliorated them. Entry was also divisive within the Conservative Party, and was strongly opposed by a minority of MPs.

The greatest problem of all was the conflict between the government and the trade union movement, then at the height of its solidarity and strength. The collisions were due to the impact of the rising cost of living upon workers' incomes, whilst the government's strategy to curb inflation required keeping wage increases down. The result was a series of industrial disputes, especially in the nationalised industries, and the Heath government declared more states of emergency than all previous governments added together. In most cases, the government had to concede more than it wished, in particular to the coal miners in February

1972. These economic issues became entangled with the trade union movement's opposition to one of the government's key measures, the Industrial Relations Act of 1971. This was intended to regulate the conduct of strikes, but the unions were adamantly opposed to any interference with free collective bargaining and refused to register under the Act. In November 1972, after talks with the employers and the trade unions on a voluntary system broke down, the government imposed a short-term freeze of wages and prices. This was followed by a system of statutory controls in which pay rises were limited to a fixed level, and for much of 1973 this was effectively maintained. However, by the end of that year inflationary pressures were mounting again, due partly to rising world commodity prices and in particular the large increase in the price of oil which followed the Arab–Israeli War of November 1973. The coal miners tabled a claim for a 35 per cent pay rise, which the government could not afford to concede without wrecking its economic strategy. The miners began an overtime ban and coal stocks at the power stations fell; to conserve energy, the government introduced blackouts and restricted industry to a three-day working week. This held the position for a while, but on 4 February 1974 a ballot of miners voted for an all-out strike, and the government played its only remaining card. Parliament was dissolved, and the following general election was fought on the theme of 'Who Governs Britain?' However, Heath wished to avoid a confrontational tone and emphasised the importance of maintaining the incomes policy, and the election posters featured the title of the party's manifesto: 'Firm action for a fair Britain'.

This appeal was unsuccessful: Heath lost his majority, and the result was a hung parliament. Although the Conservative Party had polled more votes, they had only 297 MPs to Labour's 301, with the balance held by the 14 Liberal MPs, 7 Scottish and 2 Welsh nationalists, and the 12 MPs from Northern Ireland. Labour returned to power as a minority administration, and it was clear that another election could not be far away – a fact which muted internal Conservative criticism and pressure for a change of leader. In October 1974, Wilson dissolved Parliament again; Labour gained some seats, having 319 MPs to the Conservatives' 277, but, with the minor parties now totalling 39 MPs, its overall majority in the House of Commons was only 3. Wilson had concluded a voluntary 'Social Contract' with the trade unions, and at first this seemed to bring industrial peace. Slightly better terms were negotiated for Britain's membership of the EEC, and Wilson was thus able to recommend a 'Yes' vote in the referendum held in June 1975, which endorsed these by a 2:1 majority. In March 1976, on reaching the age of 60, Wilson retired from the premiership and was succeeded by James Callaghan. Later in that year, economic problems led to pressure on the pound, and the government was forced to seek emergency support from the International Monetary Fund. During the next two years, the government had to implement cuts in spending, and industrial relations continued to be difficult. However, the situation seemed to be improving, and Callaghan decided not to call an election in the autumn of 1978, when it was widely expected, but to wait for the following spring. This prove to be a fatal error: the continuing high inflation fuelled pent-up wage demands, especially of local government workers, and led to the strikes of the 'Winter of Discontent'. After its majority was eroded through by-election defeats, the government lost a vote of confidence on 28 March 1979, and Callaghan called a general election for 3 May.

In February 1975, Heath had been forced to hold a ballot for the party leadership, in which he was defeated by the unexpected challenge of Margaret Thatcher. Her election marked a move to the right for the Conservative Party, especially on economic policy. Thatcher also adopted a populist style, advocating 'housewife economics' – that the country, like any family, could not afford to live beyond its means. The government's economic record had been the subject of sustained attack, and the record post-war level of unemployment made it vulnerable. This was the theme of an effective poster campaign devised by the rising advertising agency to which Thatcher had entrusted the party account, Saatchi & Saatchi. The famous 'Labour isn't working' poster first appeared as part of a pre-emptive campaign for the possible autumn 1978 election, and was used again in the actual contest in the spring. The outcome of this was a definite victory for the Conservatives: they won 339 seats to 269 for Labour, with 11 Liberals and 16 from the minor parties; this gave Britain's first woman prime minister a small but sufficient overall majority.

Firm action for a fair Britain
VOTE CONSERVATIVE

**FIRM ACTION
FOR A FAIR BRITAIN (1974)**

This was the slogan in the February 1974 general election, and was repeated on other posters.

1974-03

IT'S LEAPFROG TO DISASTER (1974)

This poster from the February 1974 election campaign focuses on the link between pay increases and rising inflation, and particularly the problem that one sector of industry gaining a rise led to competing demands by others seeking to maintain their differentials; this had been a key factor leading to the coal strikes of 1972 and 1974.

1974-05

It's leapfrog to disaster.
Without a fair pay and prices policy.

Firm action for a fair Britain
VOTE CONSERVATIVE

PRICES ARE NOW RISING TWICE AS FAST AS LAST YEAR – THE PLUG (1974)

1974-12B

PRICES ARE NOW RISING TWICE AS FAST AS LAST YEAR – THE SHOPPING TROLLEY (1974)

1974-14

Having lost office after the February 1974 election, in the general election of October 1974 the Conservatives were able to attack Labour's record.

128

PUT BRITAIN FIRST (1974)

1974-18

LABOUR ISN'T WORKING (1978)

Probably the most famous Conservative poster image of them all, and referenced several times in following decades, this poster was a result of the involvement of the cutting-edge advertising agency Saatchi & Saatchi in the party's campaigning by the new Conservative leader, Margaret Thatcher; the queue for the photo shoot was provided by local Conservative Party members from the north London suburban constituencies of Brent North and Hendon. The poster refers to the rise in unemployment and was prepared when it was expected that the Labour prime minister, James Callaghan, would call a general election in the autumn of 1978; in the event, he waited until the spring of 1979, and the poster was used again then in various formats.

1978-01

**DON'T JUST HOPE
FOR A BETTER LIFE (1978)**

The Conservative leader,
Margaret Thatcher, together
with a slogan which sums up
one of the elements of what
came to be called 'Thatcherism'.

1978 9-03

CHEER UP! (1978)

The poster refers to Labour's position as a minority government, at this time being maintained in office as a result of a pact with the Liberal Party.

1978/9-08

EDUCASHUN ISNT WURKING (1978)

The slogan echoes the 'Labour isn't working' theme, and focuses here upon declining standards in spelling and grammar, and the issue of comprehensive education.

1978/9-09

OPPOSITE

LABOUR STILL ISN'T WORKING (1979)

This reissue of the highly successful original poster was intended to maintain its impact; in fact, this was the version that was most widely used and that was seen by most people.

1978/9-10

BRITAIN ISN'T GETTING ANY BETTER (1979)

Another use of the same queue image, in this case attacking growing hospital waiting lists in the National Health Service.

1978/9-12

TAX.
THE FACTS.

In the last 30 years, every Labour Government has increased income tax.

Every Conservative Government has cut income tax.

This Labour Government has more than <u>doubled</u> the income tax paid by the average household.

VOTE CONSERVATIVE X

PRICES.
THE FACTS.

Since the war, prices have gone up twice as much with Labour Governments as they have with Conservative Governments.

Prices have <u>doubled</u> since this Labour Government came to power in 1974.

VOTE CONSERVATIVE X

PRICES (1979)

1978⁄9-19

TAX (1979)

1978⁄9-20

1984 (1979)

This poster from the 1979
general election campaign plays
on the reference to George
Orwell's famous novel, and on
the contemporary feeling that
government was increasingly
controlling aspects of people's
lives. 'Britain's better off with
the Conservatives' was the
campaign slogan used generally
in Conservative propaganda in
1978–79.

1978/9-11

1984

WHAT WOULD BRITAIN BE LIKE AFTER
ANOTHER 5 YEARS OF LABOUR GOVERNMENT?

BRITAIN'S BETTER OFF WITH THE CONSERVATIVES.

THE TRIUMPH OF THATCHERISM

Mrs Thatcher was the dominant political personality in Britain throughout the 1980s, and the ideas and policies associated with her were distinctive enough that they became known as 'Thatcherism'. This was primarily an economic policy, based on reducing the role of the state by removing controls and returning nationalised industries to private ownership, and instead promoting the role of free markets. The aims were to encourage enterprise (especially small businesses), to create a more flexible labour market and to offer consumers greater choice. The impact of Thatcher was such that these became the defining issues of British politics, with an influence that outlasted her tenure as prime minister and played a substantial part in shaping the 'New Labour' of Tony Blair. However, at first things were not so successful, and it seemed that the Conservative government might last only a single term – if even that. In her first government, the prime minister and her chancellor of the exchequer, Sir Geoffrey Howe, followed the approach advocated by revisionist economists such as Milton Friedman; this was based upon using the money supply to regulate the economy and control inflation. In Howe's budgets of 1979–82, public expenditure was cut and income tax reduced, but indirect taxes – in particular, Value Added Tax – were increased. Interest rates were raised, and the economy went into recession, with unemployment rising from just over 1 million when the government took office to the record level of 3 million in January 1982. This led to strains within the cabinet, and to the breaking of another record, as Thatcher's approval rating as prime minister plunged to 23 per cent at the end of 1980.

Thatcherism was a conscious rejection of post-war 'consensus politics', and the prime minister's personal style was one of confronting opposition directly, whether this was at home or abroad. Her strong stance on nuclear

defence in the Cold War earned her the label of 'the Iron Lady', and she played up to this image in her speech to the 1980 party conference, when the economic outlook was bleak, with a reminder of the problems of the Heath government: 'U-turn if you want to – the lady's not for turning!' She rode out the problems of 1980–81, which included race riots in the inner cities and a cabinet crisis which led to the sacking or marginalisation of the main opponents of the monetarist strategy, known as the 'wets'. The founding of the Social Democratic Party by four former Labour cabinet ministers in 1981, and its subsequent partnership with the Liberals in the 'Alliance', attracted many moderate voters; for a while, it led in the opinion polls and won by-elections in safe Conservative seats. However, the SDP was much more a sign of the problems of the Labour opposition than of the unpopularity of the Conservative government. The Labour Party seemed to have swung to the left since 1980, with the election of Michael Foot as its leader, the rising influence of Tony Benn and the far left, the entryism of the Marxist 'Militant Tendency', and the revival of the Campaign for Nuclear Disarmament. By 1983, Labour was committed to withdrawal from the EEC, unilateral nuclear disarmament, widespread nationalisations, abolition of the House of Lords and a range of left-wing policies, all of which provided easy targets to attack. Most importantly, by 1982 there were signs of economic improvement and a revival of confidence, especially in the financial sector. Whilst inflation had risen to 22 per cent in 1980, by the spring of 1983 it had been reduced to 4 per cent. The trade union reforms, the privatisation programme and the sale of council houses to their tenants all had popular appeal, and to this was added the 'Falklands factor' – the boost from victory in the conflict which resulted from the Argentinian invasion of the Falkland Islands, in which Thatcher's resolute leadership increased her international prestige and domestic popularity.

The Conservative Party was already eighteen points ahead of Labour in the opinion polls when Thatcher called the general election in June 1983. The result was a landslide victory, with the Conservatives winning 397 seats whilst Labour – who were almost wiped out in southern England – were reduced to 209. With the Liberal/SDP Alliance held at 23, and 21 seats for the minor parties, Thatcher now had the weight of an overall majority of 144 behind her. The second term saw the pushing ahead with previous policies, with further privatisations including British Telecom and British Gas, and tax cuts, which led to a boom under the new chancellor of the exchequer, Nigel Lawson. The government successfully withstood the challenge of a year-long coal strike in 1984–85 and an internal dispute over the future of the Westland helicopter company, which caused the resignation of the defence secretary, Michael Heseltine, in January 1986. During these years, the economy expanded and incomes rose, inflation was low and unemployment fell, although pockets of high unemployment remained in the inner cities and the old heavy industry areas.

In March 1987, Lawson's budget reduced the basic rate of income tax by two pence, and a few days later the Conservative Party's Central Council called for an early general election to capitalise on this. In April, Thatcher returned from a high-profile visit to Russia, now led by the reformist president Mikhail Gorbachev, and election speculation mounted. When it was held in June, four years after the 1983 landslide, the Conservatives were once again riding high in the polls and there was little expectation that they could lose. Although an effective television party broadcast focusing on the Labour leader, Neil Kinnock, caused some alarm during the campaign, the result was a comfortable victory. There was a feeling that Britain had shown the world a new recipe for economic success and was being regarded by other countries as the example to follow, and Thatcher had considerable worldwide prestige. This was highlighted in the election posters, with the slogan 'Britain is great again. Don't let Labour wreck it' echoing the last period of such confident affluence in 1959. The Conservatives retained most of their 1983 landslide, losing only 21 seats; the final tally was 376 Conservative seats, 229 Labour, 22 Liberal/SDP Alliance and 23 for the minor parties, leaving Thatcher a majority of 102.

**UNEMPLOYMENT –
BRITAIN'S WEATHERING
THE STORM BETTER (1983)**

This poster defends the
employment record of the
first Thatcher government of
1979–83 by pointing out that the
deep recession was a worldwide
occurrence, and comparing the
position with the main economic
competitors.

1983-08

140

FOOT PUMP (1983)

The caption refers to the Labour leader, Michael Foot, and the likelihood that Labour's economic and trade union policies would stoke inflation; the suggestion that the balloon was filled with hot air is a reference to Foot's tendency to long and rambling answers to questions.

1983-04

LABOUR –
THE OPPOSITION PARTY
(1983)

The infighting within the Labour Party in opposition after 1979, which also led to a break away of MPs to form the Social Democratic Party, provided the Conservatives with an easy target; the 'Punch and Judy' puppets are the prominent left-winger Tony Benn (appropriately, on the left) and the Labour leader Michael Foot (on the right)

1983-09

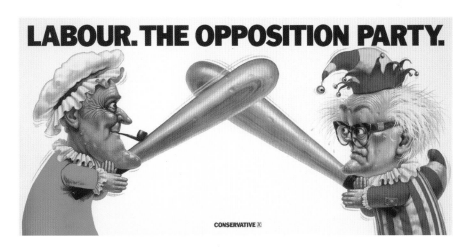

AND NOW, THE THOUGHTS OF COMRADE WALL.

"A Marxist Labour Government would have to carry through a Socialist transformation of society… over a very short period of time.

It would mean the abolition of the Monarchy, the House of Lords, the sacking of Generals, the Admirals, the Air Marshals, the senior Civil Servants, the Police Chiefs, and in particular the Judges and people of that character.

If that were not done we will get violence in Britain.

We will face the possibility in Britain of a civil war and the terrible deaths and destruction and bloodshed that would mean."

PAT WALL, LABOUR CANDIDATE BRADFORD NORTH, MAR 7th '82.

Mr Foot travels to Bradford today to endorse and support Mr Wall. Is *this* the Labour party that deserves your vote?

CONSERVATIVE X

AND NOW, THE THOUGHTS OF COMRADE WALL (1983)

Another easy target was the statements of members of Labour's 'hard left', one such example being Pat Wall, a leading figure in the Trotskyist 'Militant Tendency'.

1983-14

WHAT ARE THE
SDP'S POLICIES? (1983)

The rise in popularity of the
Social Democratic Party,
formed by four former Labour
cabinet ministers in 1981, and
its appeal to middle-class voters
in particular, was a matter of
concern for the Conservative
Party in the 1983 general
election; the featuring of ten
bottles of claret as the 'prize'
was a dig at the leader of the
SDP, Roy Jenkins, who was
known to enjoy fine wines.

1983-07

TEN BOTTLES OF CLARET CAN BE WON FOR THE BEST GUESS. WRITE TO CONSERVATIVE CENTRAL OFFICE, 32 SMITH SQUARE, LONDON SW1P 3HH.

The poster refers to the level of
local government expenditure
by Labour councils, and
the putting of services such
as refuse collection out to
competitive tender.

1983-11

EVEN WHEN
CONSERVATIVES
TALK RUBBISH
IT MAKES SENSE.

BIRMINGHAM CONSERVATIVE COUNCIL SAVED £3,000,000 ON REFUSE COLLECTION.
WIRRAL CONSERVATIVE COUNCIL SAVED £1,400,000 ON REFUSE COLLECTION.
WANDSWORTH CONSERVATIVE COUNCIL SAVED £3,000,000 ON REFUSE COLLECTION.
THESE ARE JUST THREE OF THE MANY CONSERVATIVE COUNCILS
THAT ARE SAVING MILLIONS OF POUNDS A YEAR ON REFUSE COLLECTION.
VOTE CONSERVATIVE.

WHO FIGHTS HARDEST FOR BRITAIN IN EUROPE? (1984)

The poster refers to Thatcher's successful fight to reduce the size of Britain's contribution to the EEC budget.

1984-02

NOW WE'VE THE FASTEST GROWTH OF ANY MAJOR ECONOMY IN EUROPE.

CONSERVATIVE ☒

THE FASTEST GROWTH OF ANY MAJOR ECONOMY (1987)

The poster highlights the turnaround in the relative performance of the European economies, contrasting the iconic British bulldog (on the right, naturally) with the French poodle (left) and the German alsation (centre).

1987-09

BRITAIN IS GREAT AGAIN (1987)

The slogan refers to the rise of confidence during the height of Thatcherism and the feeling that Britain was setting an example to the world; the subtitle 'Don't let Labour wreck it' was an echo of the iconic poster of 1959, when there was also a Conservative government seeking re-election during a period of rising real incomes and living standards.

1987-14

BRITAIN
NOW HAS
THE FEWEST
STRIKES
FOR
50 YEARS.

**The last Labour Government ended in
The Winter of Discontent.**

BRITAIN IS GREAT AGAIN. DON'T LET LABOUR WRECK IT.
VOTE CONSERVATIVE ☒

BRITAIN
IS GREAT
AGAIN.
DON'T LET
LABOUR
WRECK IT.

VOTE CONSERVATIVE ☒

BRITAIN NOW HAS THE FEWEST STRIKES FOR 50 YEARS (1987)

Following the trade union legislation of the early 1980s and the defeat of the coal strike of 1984–85, and with wage levels rising and unemployment falling, there was a notable decline in strikes compared to previous decades.

1987-15

SECONDARY PICKETING (1987)

This poster is a reminder of the aspect of strikes which has led to violent confrontation in the past, and is an example of the speed with which the Conservative publicity machine could react – in this case, to a comment made on television by the leader of the Labour Party, Neil Kinnock, a few days earlier.

1987-22

LABOUR'S POLICY ON ARMS.

CONSERVATIVE ⊠
THE NEXT MOVE FORWARD

**LABOUR'S POLICY ON ARMS
(1987)**

This is an iconic poster from the 1987 general election, with the play on words referring to the influence within the Labour Party of supporters of unilateral nuclear disarmament.

1987-08

10,500 MORE POLICEMEN ARE HELPING THE POLICE WITH THEIR ENQUIRIES.

CONSERVATIVE ⊠
THE NEXT MOVE FORWARD

**10,500 MORE POLICEMEN
(1987)**

Concern over rising crime rates was an important issue in the 1980s, and so the increased level of police manpower was a political advantage to be publicised.

1987-10

**IS THIS LABOUR'S IDEA OF A
COMPREHENSIVE EDUCATION?
(1987)**

The poster refers to well-
publicised examples of Labour
local authorities, particularly
in Central London, adopting
policies in education and public
library provision which were
seen in some quarters to be
anti-police and to encourage
teenage sexual promiscuity
and homosexuality; this led
after the Conservative victory
to legislation banning local
government funds from being
used in these ways.

1987-07

IS THIS LABOUR'S IDEA OF A COMPREHENSIVE EDUCATION?

Young gay & proud.

Police: Out of School!

The playbook for kids about sex.

TAKE THE POLITICS OUT OF EDUCATION. VOTE CONSERVATIVE ☒

SO THIS IS THE NEW MODERATE MILITANT-FREE LABOUR PARTY (1987)

Despite efforts by the Labour leader, Neil Kinnock, to purge his party of entryist factions, the continuing presence of supporters of the Trotskyist 'Militant Tendency' group, and its sympathisers, gave the Conservative Party easy targets to attack.

1987-23

Published by C.C.F., 32 Smith Square, London, SW1P 3HH
Printed by Orchard & Ind Ltd., 104 Northgate Street, Gloucester, GL1 1SP

ONE ALLIANCE, TWO IDEOLOGIES (1987)

The 'Alliance' of the Liberal Party and the Social Democratic Party was still popular, but there were tensions within it and the public remained unclear about its programme.

1987-03

THE NEW DIRECTION? (1987)

1987-04

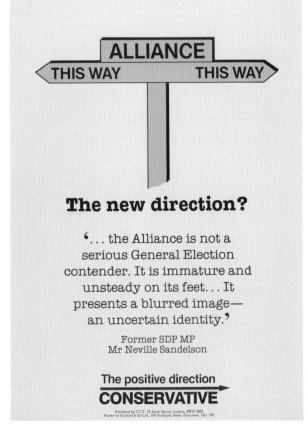

Published by C.C.F., 32 Smith Square, London, SW1P 3HH
Printed by Orchard & Ind Ltd., 104 Northgate Street, Gloucester, GL1 1SP

DIVISIONS AND DEFEATS

Thatcher had won an unprecedented third successive term as prime minister in 1987, and was determined to press forward with even greater reforming vigour. However, her confidence was to contribute to her downfall, in two key areas. The first of these was the long-promised reform of local government finance, which replaced the property-based rates with a new universal flat-rate citizen charge, which was promptly dubbed the 'poll tax'. This aroused considerable opposition, but its problems were largely a reflection of the wider economic picture. In 1988, when it seemed the government could do all things, Lawson reduced the higher rate tax band from 60 per cent to 40 per cent, and the lower rate by a further two pence to 25 per cent. Initially popular, this led to a runaway boom in house prices and rising inflation, and then to recession at the end of the decade. Against this background, Thatcher's inflexibility over the 'poll tax' and the Conservative Party's consequent unpopularity alarmed MPs in marginal seats, and they began to see the prime minister as a liability rather than an asset. At the same time, her assertiveness in the second area – relations with Europe – shattered key relationships within the leadership, with Lawson resigning in October 1989 and Geoffrey Howe in November 1990. The latter event led to a challenge to Thatcher's leadership from Michael Heseltine, and her failure to secure outright victory in the first ballot and opposition to her continuing to the second round from the cabinet led to her resignation.

The successor to emerge from the resulting leadership contest was the relatively unknown figure of John Major, as he was the candidate thought most able to unify a divided and traumatised party. Major had been endorsed by Thatcher, but proved to be a moderate pragmatist. At first, this enabled him to distance his government from Thatcher's and to follow more

LOWEST INFLATION FOR 50 YEARS.

With the longest period of low inflation for 50 years, the outlook for Britain has never looked brighter. But remember: New Labour New Danger.

CONSERVATIVE

popular policies, including abandoning the 'poll tax'. This thorny task was given to Heseltine, who joined the cabinet and established a strong working relationship with Major, eventually becoming deputy prime minister in 1995. Major had an even humbler background than Thatcher, coming from the inner-city Brixton district of London, and this theme was promoted in party television broadcasts and posters. He was personally popular, and although criticised in some quarters as too 'grey' and low-key, the contrast with the often abrasive Thatcher was beneficial. Major called the election in April 1992, a few months before the maximum term of the parliament. He was expected to lose, but he fought doggedly, with his 'man in the street' image highlighted by impromptu public speeches given standing on an old-fashioned soapbox. With the recession worsening, the party's national campaign concentrated on negative attacks on Labour and featured a number of striking poster images, particularly 'Labour's Tax Bombshell' and 'Labour's Double Whammy'. These focused on Labour's tax plans and, together with strong support from popular newspapers such as *The Sun* and a prematurely triumphalist performance from Kinnock at Labour's final rally in Sheffield, they shifted public opinion a decisive few points towards the Conservatives in the last days of the contest. The unexpected result was a narrow Conservative win, with 336 MPs to 271 for Labour, 20 for the now-merged Liberal Democrats, and 24 for the other parties.

Major thus remained in office, with an overall majority of 21. At first, this seemed sufficient to govern, but it dwindled away during the next five years through by-election defeats and defections. This left the government dangerously vulnerable to a handful of rebel 'Euro-sceptic' MPs, and resulted in a long and debilitating struggle in 1992–93 over the ratification of the Maastricht Treaty. Encouraged by Thatcher, whose off-stage interventions complicated Major's problems, serious rifts opened up within the Conservative Party over the issue of Europe; this became so corrosive that Major called a leadership election in June 1995 to reimpose his authority. The Major government of 1992–97 was a painful period for the Conservative Party, and its opinion poll ratings slumped to record lows following the economic fiasco of 'Black Wednesday' in September 1992, when sterling had to leave the European Exchange Rate Mechanism.

Major's speech to the 1993 party conference on the theme of 'back to basics' was misinterpreted as a call for traditional morality; it appeared hypocritical, as over the following years the press exposed a series of personal scandals involving Conservative ministers and MPs, which became known as 'sleaze'. However, the worst problems once again related to the economy. The recession of the early 1990s hit hard in areas of traditional Conservative support in the south, and led to some spectacular by-election losses to the Liberal Democrats. More dangerously, 'New Labour' under Tony Blair was adroitly heading for the middle ground. By 1995 the economic picture was improving and unemployment falling, but the government was deeply unpopular and earned no credit from this. Major postponed the election to the last possible date, with polling on 1 May 1997. The outcome was the third heavy defeat of the century, and 178 MPs – including seven cabinet ministers – were swept away by the Labour landslide. The result gave Labour 418 MPs and a majority of 177 over the 165 Conservatives, 46 Liberal Democrats (who had also done well out of the Conservative defeat), and 30 others.

Major resigned on the day after the poll; his successor, William Hague, was the youngest Conservative leader in modern times at the age of 36. However, the party remained unpopular, whilst the Labour government's careful management of the economy meant that it survived any other difficulties without lasting damage. Hague was an effective debater in the House of Commons, but struggled to establish a clear position for the party with the public, and attempts to present a more modern and casual image had little effect. He followed a more 'Euro-sceptic' policy, ruling out joining the single European currency; this caused tensions in the party but also led to its greatest success in the period, doubling its seats to 36 in the European Parliament elections of June 1999. However, concentration on Europe was less effective in the June 2001 general election, and Conservative hopes of at least a partial recovery were dashed. In an unprecedented result, Labour held on to almost all of the seats gained in its 1997 landslide: the Conservatives gained only a single seat, returning 166 MPs to Labour's 415, whilst the Liberal Democrats increased their representation to 52.

IN COME LABOUR.

In an effort to get into power, Labour has made billions of pounds worth of promises. But they haven't told you where the money is coming from. Because they suspect you won't like the answer. See below.

INCOME TAXES.

£10,000	SECRETARY Single	£796 MORE under Labour	£20,000	TEACHER Married, 2 children, mortgage.	£1272 MORE under Labour
£14,000	NURSE Single	£1296 MORE under Labour	£24,000	ENGINEER Married, 2 children, mortgage.	£2037 MORE under Labour
£17,500	ELECTRICIAN Married, 2 children, mortgage.	£960 MORE under Labour	£25,000	JOURNALIST Married with mortgage	£2379 MORE under Labour

It's obvious to everyone but Labour – high taxes would destroy incentive and cripple recovery. Conservatives want taxes as low as possible to put more money in people's pockets, create more demand and more jobs.

CONSERVATIVE ⊠

IN COME LABOUR (1992)

The central theme of the Conservative campaign in the 1992 general election was that income tax levels would rise again under a Labour government.

1992-01

EVERYTHING BRITAIN
HAS WON (1992)

Another theme of the campaign was that the achievements of the Conservative governments since 1979, such as low inflation and investment by overseas companies, would be lost under Labour; point 7 features an early use of the phrase 'back to basics'.

1992–03

EVERYTHING
BRITAIN
HAS WON

1. Britain has gone from being the sick man of Europe to being a world leader again.

2. Today, we have lower inflation than most of our European competitors. This is the key to making Britain even more competitive, the edge we need to help us move ahead as we come out of recession.

3. We believe in giving everyone the maximum incentive to work hard, and the freedom to choose how they spend their own money. So we have brought personal taxes down, and introduced a new 20p band particularly to help the low paid. Our aim is to gradually move more and more people to the 20p in the £ level.

4. Today overseas companies invest more in Britain than in any other country in Europe. They came because we are now a strike-free, low inflation, hard working country. That's why 87% of leading businessmen want a Conservative government to manage the economy.

5. Without creating a wealthy Britain, we could never have afforded the massive rises in spending on welfare and public services we have seen in the last decade.

6. The NHS has seen its budget grow from £8bn to £36bn under the Conservatives. Today, over a million more people a year are treated in NHS hospitals and waiting lists are coming down and down.

7. We are raising standards in schools, by getting back to basics, and by giving more choice and power

to parents. Twice as many children are now going on to higher education.

8. Strikes used to be a way of life in Britain. Our trade union reforms took power from union bosses and put it in the hands of the people. Now we have the lowest level of strikes for 100 years.

9. Much has been achieved. But Britain is understandably frustrated because the world recession is making life tough and uncertain. Today we are better placed than our competitors to gain maximum advantage as the world recession fades.

10. Britain's living standards have never been higher than during the Conservative years.

Don't allow all the achievements of the last decade to be swept away.

Everything Britain has won, Labour would lose.

LABOUR
WOULD LOSE.

CONSERVATIVE ☒

157

**YOU CAN ONLY BE SURE
WITH THE CONSERVATIVES
(1992)**

This poster features John
Major, who became leader of the
Conservative Party in November
1990 after the fall of Margaret
Thatcher.

1992-19

YOU CAN
ONLY BE SURE
WITH THE
CONSERVATIVES

Printed & published by Conservative Central Office, 32 Smith Square, Westminster, London SW1P 3HH

A WORKING CLASS KID FROM BRIXTON (1992)

This poster highlights Major's upbringing in inner-city London, after the failure of his father's business (in reality, Major's family background was not working class).

1992–07

VOTE FOR RECOVERY.

NOT THE START OF A NEW RECESSION.

Just as recovery is under way, Labour would start a new recession. A Conservative win will end uncertainty, raise confidence and speed Britain ahead. Labour would put taxes up, mortgages up, inflation up and strikes up. That's why 90% of business leaders say that Britain needs the Conservatives to keep Britain moving forward.

VOTE CONSERVATIVE ☒

WHAT DOES THE CONSERVATIVE PARTY OFFER A WORKING CLASS KID FROM BRIXTON?

THEY MADE HIM PRIME MINISTER.

No wonder John Major believes everyone should have an equal opportunity.

CONSERVATIVE ☒

VOTE FOR RECOVERY (1992)

In fact, the recession of the early 1990s became worse after the election, and its impact in the Conservative heartlands of southern England was crucial in the party's loss of popularity after 1992 and the landslide defeat of 1997.

1992–04

159

YOU CAN'T TRUST LABOUR (1992)

The use of the learner-driver L-plate was intended to remind voters of Labour's inexperience due to its long period in opposition.

1992-09

LABOUR IN. EVERYBODY OUT! (1992)

This poster refers to Labour intentions to repeal much of the trade union legislation of the Thatcher era, which it is suggested will return the country to the pre-1979 level of industrial disputes.

1992-10

OPPOSITE

LABOUR'S DOUBLE WHAMMY (1992)

This is one of the two iconic images from the 1992 election campaign, both of which focused on the prospect of higher taxes under a Labour government.

1992-13

LABOUR'S TAX BOMBSHELL (1992)

The second of the iconic posters of 1992.

1992-15

160

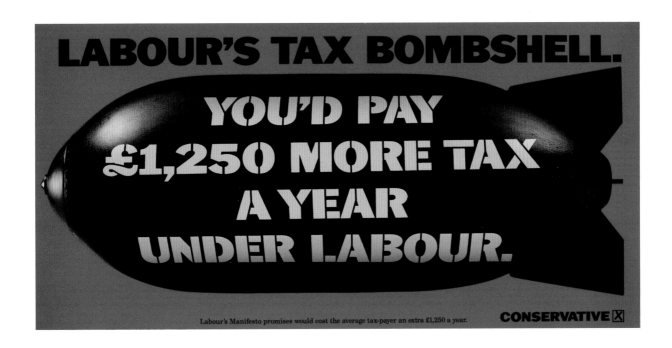

162

YES IT HURT –
YES IT WORKED (1997)

The poster acknowledges the impact of the recession of the early 1990s, defending the policies that followed as having led to recovery.

1997-21

BRITAIN IS BOOMING (1997)

The Major government could point to an improving economic picture by 1997, but public opinion did not perceive this or give the government any credit for it; on this occasion, unlike in 1959 and 1987, many voters did not regard the Conservatives as delivering prosperity, and therefore the suggestion that Labour would threaten this was far less effective.

1997-01

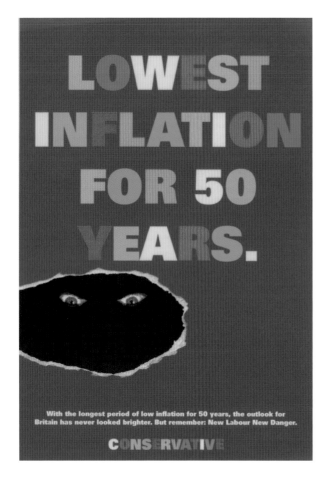

**LOWEST INFLATION FOR
50 YEARS (1997)**

The use of the 'demon eyes'
image was a feature of this
series of posters and of several
others in the 1997 campaign; for
the original and definitive use
of this device, see 'New Labour,
New Danger' at the front of the
book.

1997–24

**LOWEST MORTGAGE RATES
FOR 30 YEARS (1997)**

1997–23

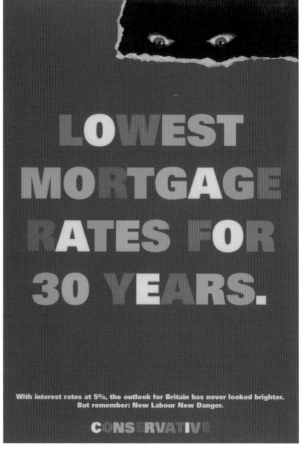

**NEW LABOUR NEW TAXES
(1997)**

1997-06

TONY & BILL (1997)

The poster features the leader
of the Labour Party, Tony Blair,
and the Conservative Party's
costings of Labour's manifesto
pledges.

1997-05

AS PROMISED (1997)

The poster features Major's trademark spectacles, which were instantly recognisable.

1997-31

The poster attacks the European
policies of Liberal Democrat
leader Paddy Ashdown, who is
pictured.

1997-35

**IN EUROPE,
NOT RUN BY EUROPE (1999)**

This poster was an attempt
to bridge the widening gap
between pro-European Union
figures in the Conservative
Party and the rising tide of
Euroscepticism at the party's
grassroots.

1999–01

In Europe,
not run
by Europe

Conservatives

Published by the Conservative Party, 32 Smith Square, London SW1P 3HH & printed by Belmont Press, Sheaf Close, Lodge Farm Industrial Estate, Harlestone Road, Northampton NN5 7UX

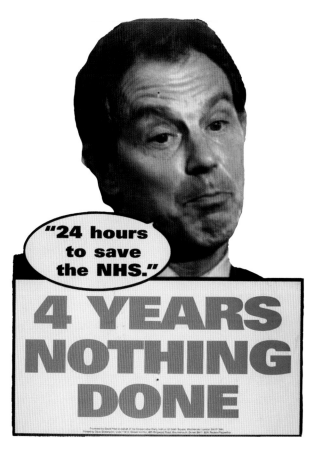

4 YEARS NOTHING DONE
(2001)

The poster attacks the record of
the Labour leader, Tony Blair,
as prime minister.

2001-06

LABOUR'S HIGHWAY ROBBERY
(2001)

The rise in petrol prices became
an issue of public concern in the
first decade of the twenty-first
century; the poster features
the Labour chancellor of the
exchequer, Gordon Brown.

2001-03

WHAT WILL LABOUR THROW YOUR MONEY AWAY ON NEXT? (2001)

The poster refers to the controversial and expensive Millennium Dome, built for the millennial celebrations, which is shown as the lid of the dustbin; it has since become the O2 Arena.

2001-05

**POLICE NUMBERS ARE DOWN
UNDER LABOUR (2001)**

2001-04

**STOP THE LIB-DEMS
TRASHING BRITAIN (2001)**

Under William Hague's
leadership in 1997–2001, the
Conservative Party adopted a
more Eurosceptic tone and ruled
out joining the single currency.

2001-01

THE LONG ROAD
BACK TO POWER

As was now customary, Hague announced his resignation on the morning
after the 2001 defeat. A new selection procedure had been introduced, and
after ballots of Conservative MPs the two leading candidates went forward
to a vote of the party membership in September 2001, from which Iain
Duncan Smith emerged the winner. During the following two years, there
was little sign of improvement in the Conservative Party's fortunes, as the
domestic political and economic situation remained largely unchanged. The
Conservatives supported the policy of Prime Minister Tony Blair in the
overthrow of Saddam Hussein's regime in Iraq in the spring and summer
of 2003. This was in tune with Conservative opinion, whilst the Labour
Party was deeply divided over the issue, but the war did not change the
relative popularity of the two parties. A significant minority of Conservative
MPs had been doubtful about Duncan Smith's leadership from the outset,
and the lack of improvement in the party's position caused this number
to increase during the summer and autumn of 2003. The criticism and
speculation culminated in a vote of confidence by Conservative MPs on
29 October, which Duncan Smith lost by 75 votes to 90. The desire of the
party to avoid further disunity was shown when only one candidate was
nominated for the vacant leadership, and so a contest was avoided. Michael
Howard was declared Leader on 6 November; although older than both of
his predecessors, he had the asset of considerable experience of government,
having been a cabinet minister from 1990 to 1997.

Howard was more effective than Duncan Smith had been in the House
of Commons, and under his leadership the party was more cohesive and
disciplined, but its standing in the opinion polls did not improve. The
economic policies of the Labour government, under which control of
interest rates had been devolved to the Bank of England in 1997, were

providing low inflation and unemployment rates together with substantial spending, particularly on health and education. Against this background, Blair was confident of success when he called the general election in May 2005, despite the unpopularity of the war in Iraq. The Conservative campaign sought to highlight the increases in indirect taxation and the failure to raise allowances in line with inflation, which were dubbed 'stealth taxes', and in particular to attack the government's record on immigration, crime and the management of the health service. The continuing problems of the occupation of Iraq were more difficult territory, but a number of posters focused on the theme of Blair having misled the country over the need for the initial invasion, and they also referenced the well-publicised rivalry within the government between the prime minister and his chancellor of the exchequer, Gordon Brown. (Regrettably, the Archive does not have copies of any posters from the 2005 general election.) The slogan of the Conservative campaign was 'Are you thinking what we're thinking?', but it seemed that most of the voters were not. The party was still burdened by the unpopularity of the Thatcher–Major years and the persistent legacy of being seen as the 'uncaring' or even 'nasty' party, and the continuing disagreements over Europe and the presence of Howard as leader made it difficult to shed this image. The Conservative share of the vote rose by less than 1 per cent, and it was the decline in Labour support which produced 33 gains for the Conservatives and 11 for the Liberal Democrats. This made some inroads upon the massive Labour lead of 1997 and 2001, but with 355 MPs to the 198 Conservatives, 62 Liberal Democrats and 31 others, Labour still retained a substantial overall majority of 64.

Howard announced his retirement on the day after the poll; after a successful speech at the party conference in October, David Cameron was elected as Conservative leader in December 2005. With a young family, Cameron sought to promote a new Conservative image, emphasising better quality of public services, support for the health system, and more concern for environmental issues; a poster campaign in 2007 featured these themes against soft-coloured floral backgrounds, with an overall message of 'Vote Blue, Go Green'. His move to a more centrist position attracted criticism from Thatcherite former ministers and press columnists, but began to show results after two significant changes in the political situation. The first of these was the retirement of Blair and Brown's succession to the premiership in June 2007; the new prime minister was widely expected to call an election to secure a fresh mandate, but failed to do so – a sign of doubt which damaged his standing and which the Conservatives adroitly exploited, accusing him of 'bottling it'. Brown proved to lack the dexterity and charm which had sustained Blair, and there were growing signs of dissension over his leadership in the Labour Party for the rest of his term. However, the decisive factor was the second event: the banking crisis of 2008 and the resulting sharp depression, the worst since the 1930s. At first, Brown seemed to have acted decisively to prevent a domestic and international collapse, but the government's popularity steadily declined under the twin effects of the recession and the long-running military conflicts in Iraq and Afghanistan.

The opinion polls first showed the Conservatives ahead of Labour in October 2007, and by May 2008 this peaked at a 26-point lead. The Conservatives remained in front for the next three years, scoring successes in the London mayoral election of 2008 and in local elections. Although by early 2010 their lead had slipped back to around ten points, when the general election finally arrived in May 2010 – having been delayed to the latest possible date – there was no doubt that the Labour Party had become the underdog and an outright Conservative victory was widely expected. The effective performances of the Liberal Democrat leader, Nick Clegg, in the first televised debates held between party leaders, made a considerable impact during the campaign, and almost certainly prevented his party from losing more of the seats that they had gained in the very different circumstances of 1997–2005. Cameron's pre-election theme of the 'Big Society' did not communicate clearly to the voters, but his criticism of Labour's record and legacy – depicted as 'Broken Britain' – and pledges to cut the huge budget deficit whilst maintaining the health service were more effective. The Conservatives won 2 million more votes than Labour and made a net gain of 97 seats, one of the largest advances recorded in a single election. However, although they were the largest party with 306 seats, they were still short of a majority over the 258 Labour, 57 Liberal Democrat and 29 minor party and independent MPs. After a few days of tense negotiation, the outcome was a coalition agreement with the Liberal Democrats. Cameron took office as prime minister on 11 May, with Clegg serving as his deputy; this was the first peacetime coalition government in Britain since the 1930s.

Let down by Labour

GUN CRIME HAS DOUBLED SINCE 1997

June 10th Vote Conservatives ✗

Let down by £££abour?

66 STEALTH TAXES SINCE 1997

June 10th Vote Conservatives ✗

LET DOWN BY LABOUR (2004)

2004-08

LET DOWN BY £££ABOUR (2004)

2004-10

Conservative MEPs are happy to list Mr Blair's successes during Britain's Presidency of the European Union:

...and he's given £7 billion back to Brussels

EPP-ED

CONSERVATIVES
IN THE EUROPEAN PARLIAMENT

Published by Conservatives in the European Parliament, 25 Victoria Street, London SW1H 0DL

MR BLAIR'S SUCCESSES DURING BRITAIN'S PRESIDENCY OF THE EUROPEAN UNION (2006)

The poster attacks Prime Minister Tony Blair's record during Britain's turn to hold the presidency of the European Union, from July to December 2005, and refers to the increase in development funding for new member countries which reduced the British budget rebate by 20 per cent.

2006-04

NH YES (2007)

A more recent example of the
continuing need since the late
1940s to reassure voters about
the Conservative Party's positive
support for the National Health
Service.

2007–08

VOTE BLUE GO GREEN (2007)

Under the leadership of David
Cameron, the Conservative
Party aligned itself with a new
pro-environmental image, of
which this was the key message.

2007-10

**BETTER PUBLIC SERVICES
(2007)**

2007–01

QUALITY OF LIFE (2007)

2007–07

STRONGER FAMILIES (2007)

2007–04

GENERAL WELL-BEING (2007)

2007–05

A series of posters emphasising
broad new priorities rather
than specific measures, with a
deliberately soft image.

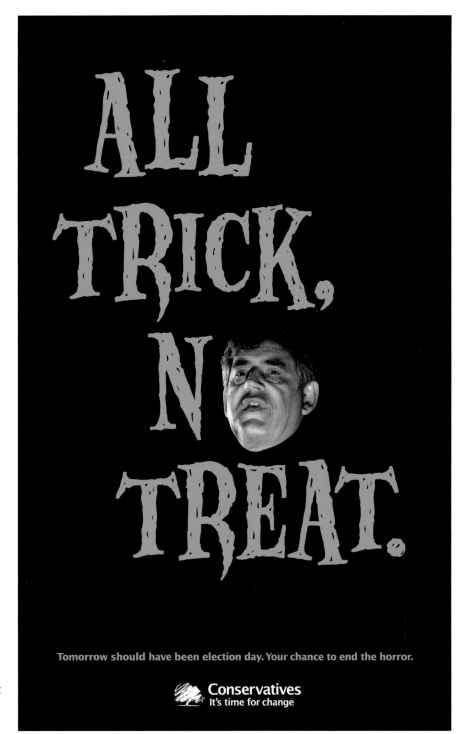

ALL TRICK, NO TREAT (2007)

The poster refers to Gordon Brown's decision not to call a general election after succeeding Tony Blair as prime minister.

2007-33

HOWEVER GORDON WRAPS IT UP, IT'S STILL A TAX BOMBSHELL.

**BROWN'S £100 BILLION BORROWING BINGE WILL MEAN HIGHER TAXES FOR YOU.
DON'T LET HIM GET AWAY WITH IT.**

www.conservatives.com

PROMOTED BY ALAN MABBUTT ON BEHALF OF THE CONSERVATIVE PARTY, BOTH OF 30 MILLBANK, LONDON SW1P 4DR.

Conservatives
It's time for change

Gordon's borrowing is criminal.

£347,945,205

By borrowing £347,945,205 every day Gordon brown is creating a whole new generation born into debt.

Conservatives

We can't go on like this.
I'll cut the deficit, not the NHS.

YEAR FOR CHANGE

Read our plan for change at conservatives.com

LET'S SCRAP ID CARDS

Vote Conservative

WE'VE GOT TO MEND OUR BROKEN SOCIETY (2010)

This is part of a series of posters under the heading 'I've never voted Tory before, but...', featuring people who would not be thought of as natural Conservative voters, generally from parts of the country which were not strongly Conservative; the 'broken society' theme was used widely by Cameron in the period 2009–10.

ACCN/2010/12

I LIKE THEIR PLANS TO HELP FAMILIES (2010)

The image of the family in this poster differs from the several previous examples, by showing only one parent.

ACCN/2010/12

I've never voted Tory before, but we've got to mend our broken society.

Find out why Danielle from Brighton is voting Tory at conservatives.com/society

I've never voted Tory before, but I like their plans to help families.

Find out why Julie from Llandudno is voting Tory at conservatives.com/families

**BROWN RECOVERY PLAN
(2010)**

ACCN/2010/54

**I DOUBLED THE NATIONAL
DEBT (2010)**

This is part of a series of posters
with statements followed by the
tag line 'Let me do it again',
and also issued with the tag line
'Vote for me'; both series used
the same picture of the Labour
prime minister, Gordon Brown.

ACCN/2010/57

GET BRITAIN WORKING (2010)

ACCN/2010/52

BYE BYE BUREAUCRACY (2010)

ACCN/2010/52

BIG SOCIETY NOT BIG GOVERNMENT (2010)

ACCN/2010/52

SOCIAL RESPONSIBILITY NOT STATE CONTROL (2010)

ACCN/2010/52

The general election campaign of 2010 featured a series of posters in a deliberately 'retro' style recalling the 1960s, with slogans evoking both long-term themes in British Conservatism on issues such as state control and bureaucracy, and the more recent concept promoted by the Conservative leader, David Cameron, of the 'big society'.